Praise for *The Cult of the Customer*

"This book reflects the core values of our approach at Morton's The Steakhouse. We not only serve The Best Steak Anywhere, but Morton's is truly focused on providing our guests with Morton's Genuine Hospitality, second to none in restaurant dining. This book is all about providing you with the necessary tools to create that amazing, top-of-the-line experience for every guest."

—Thomas J. Baldwin
Chairman, CEO and President,
Morton's Restaurant Group

"At Zappos.com, we've always recognized that customers need to be more than satisfied—they need to be WOWed! Shep recognizes this as well in his book, and gives plenty of examples of how different companies go about creating WOW experiences."

—Tony Hsieh
CEO of Zappos.com

"Brilliant! *The Cult of the Customer* is a light that shows us the way that organizations can win and keep winning!"

—Ralph Dandre
CEO of ITX Corporation

"Once again Shep has used his "magic" to make customer service easy—to understand and implement. I am definitely a member of "*The Cult of the Customer*," and once you've read this book you will be, too."

—Keith Rhodes
CFO and Senior VP of Alter Trading

"Selling mortgages is a commodity business, and that presents a real problem. How do we compete when our competition sells the same thing that we do—and at the same price? The answer is in *The Cult of the Customer*. Drink Shep's Kool-Aid. Study this book. Work through the exercises. You will gain the competitive edge you need to succeed."

—Doug Schukar
CEO, USA Mortgage

"Whatever happens on the inside of a company is also felt on the outside. This book delivers a step-by-step approach on how your company can create amazing internal experiences that directly impacts the customer."

—Jon Williams
vice-president, Good Earth Tools

"Years ago Shep Hyken defined a new standard for outstanding customer service through showing us how to create Moments of Magic. *The Cult of the Customer* expands on his previous work in ways both evolutionary and revolutionary, moving beyond "moments" to forming a culture of customer experience that creates not only advocates but "Evangelist" for you, your business and your brand. If this is your Vision then this is your book!"

—Barry Knight
President of NEXT Financial Group

"*The Cult of the Customer* is an inspiration; written in a way that all companies in all industries can relate to, and therefore benefit from, by using the tools in the book to build customer loyalty and employee evangelists, resulting in a journey toward amazement that is guaranteed to separate you from your closest competitor."

—Ken Muskat, ACC
Vice President of Sales for
Royal Caribbean International

"We sell more than Teddy Bears. What we sell are experiences and memories that last a lifetime. Get into *The Cult of the Customer* and you won't just amaze your customers; they will amaze you—with their love and passion for the experiences you create for them!"

—Maxine Clark
Chief Executive Bear, Build-A-Bear Workshop

THE CULT
OF THE
CUSTOMER

Create an Amazing Customer Experience That Turns Satisfied Customers into Customer Evangelists

Shep Hyken

WILEY

John Wiley & Sons, Inc.

Published by John Wiley & Sons, Inc., Hoboken, New Jersey
Published simultaneously in Canada

For general information on our other products and services or for technical support, please contact our Customer Care Department within the United States at (800) 762-2974, outside the United States at (317) 572-3993 or fax (317) 572-4002.

Wiley also publishes its books in a variety of electronic formats. Some content that appears in print may not be available in electronic books. For more information about Wiley products, visit our web site at www.wiley.com.

Library of Congress Cataloging-in-Publication Data:

Hyken, Shep.
  The cult of the customer: create an amazing customer experience that turns satisfied customers into customer evangelists / by Shep Hyken.
        p. cm.
  Includes index.
  ISBN 978-0-470-40482-9 (cloth)
  1. Customer services. 2. Customer loyalty. 3. Customer relations. I. Title.
  HF5415.5.H937 2009
  658.8′12—dc22

                                                2008042913

Printed in the United States of America
10 9 8 7 6 5 4 3 2 1

Contents

Read This First   *ix*

Part 1   **The Purpose of Your Business**

Chapter 1   The Genie and the Ice Cream Shop   3

Chapter 2   Do You Need This Book?   5

Chapter 3   The Three Forces   19

Part 2   **The Five Cults**

Chapter 4   Uncertainty   31

Chapter 5   Alignment   43

Chapter 6   Experience   53

Chapter 7   Ownership   63

Chapter 8   *Amazement*   73

Part 3   **The Journey to *Amazement***

Chapter 9   What the Journey Looks Like from
                   the Inside: The Internal March
                   to *Amazement*   89

Chapter 10   What the Journey Looks Like from
                   the Outside: The External March
                   to *Amazement*   105

Chapter 11   Launching the *Amazement Revolution*   123

Part 4   ***Amazement* in Action**

Chapter 12   Little Things: Snapshots of
                   Organizations and People Who Get
                   the Little Things Right   143

Chapter 13   Problem Solving and Recovery:
                   Snapshots of Organizations and People
                   Who Solve Problems and Recover Well   153

Chapter 14   Opportunity Knocks: Organizations and
                   People Who Look for Opportunities to
                   Be Better Than Average   171

Chapter 15   Proactive Service and Follow-Through:
                   Snapshots of Proactive Organizations
                   and People in Action   179

Chapter 16   The Art of WOW: Snapshots of
                   Truly *Amazing* Organizations
                   and People   189

Part 5   **Creating the Cult of the Customer**

Chapter 17   Tools for Success   205

Epilogue   *227*

Notes   *231*

Acknowledgments   *235*

About the Author   *237*

Index   *239*

Read This First

What Is the Cult of the Customer?

If you're in business, it's the cult you *want* to belong to.

First things first: There's nothing scary about the word *cult*. If you stop and think about it, you'll realize you can find the word *cult* inside words you already know and use without any problem, words like *culture* and *cultivate*. *Cult* comes from the Latin word *cultus,* which originally meant "care or tending." What we're proposing in this book is creating a corporate *culture* that is so focused on taking care of and tending to employees and customers that the culture *itself* creates evangelists.

Evangelists are special people who go out of their way to tell the world just how *great* you and your company are. They are exactly the kind of advocates that you want your organization's *culture* to create. That's the end result of *The Cult of the Customer*.

There are many companies who have managed to build a culture that has reached this level—a culture rooted in a concept called *amazement.* In this book, I'll tell you their stories, show you exactly how they made *The Cult of the Customer* happen, and show you how you can make it happen, too. You'll start by determining what cult you're in now and then by figuring out what cult you *want* to be in.

Please bear this in mind as you make your way through this book. A cult is nothing more or less than a *system of shared belief, interest, or experience*—in other words, a group of people with a shared agreement about what they will be *cultivating* together. For example, you may be passionate about bike riding and like to hang out with other cyclists on weekends. Strictly speaking, that's a cult. You may enjoy action hero comic books and attend a comic book convention twice a year. That, too, is a cult. When it comes to business, I'm in a cult, and I hope you are, too: *The Cult of the Customer!*

The Discovery

Since the mid-1980s, I've been speaking and writing about customer service, internal service, customer loyalty, the customer experience—virtually anything that had to do with building a relationship with the people with whom you work or do business. This book takes everything I've learned over the years to a higher level. It's based on a discovery I made recently; something that I've suspected for years but have only now been able to prove with the examples and principles in this book:

Employees and customers live in a parallel world.

Years ago, I identified five phases that customers go through from the time they first start doing business with you until they become loyal to you and your company. That much was set, even though the names I gave those phases changed over time. Here is the interesting part—the part that matters to you and me as business-people. Employees of your company go through *identical* phases.

For a company to create an *amazing* experience—one that creates not just loyal customers but company evangelists—the employees of that company must move through these phases *before* the customers do. These phases are the various *cults* that your company may be in. You'll learn about all these cults in this book.

A Disclaimer

Throughout this book, you will learn about the various corporate cults. I've shared stories of some great companies as positive examples of the journey to *amazement,* the ultimate *cult of the customer.* Of course, these companies are operating successfully at the time of this writing, but, like any company, they may not *continue* doing so over time. Staying in the *cult of amazement* is a difficult job; some companies pull it off, and others don't.

As I write this book, these companies are operating at the top of their game. They are great role models, because they are operating in a phase you will come to know as *amazement.* Of course, there is no guarantee that they will stay at the top.

Back in 1982, Tom Peters and Robert Waterman profiled 43 of what they called America's "best-run companies" in one of the greatest business books ever written, *In Search of Excellence.* Today, a number of those companies are no longer in existence or might not be considered, at least by their customers, to be excellent. Yet when this book came out a quarter of a century ago, these companies were, indeed, considered to be the best of the best. The businesses that I have cited as role models here are, as this book goes to press, the best role models I know of for the journey to *amazement.* That being said, I know that any given company can fall from grace quickly. I also know that even a great company—and one with legions of evangelists—has its detractors.

No person—and no organization—is perfect. It is the *pursuit* of perfection, the effort that is put into *being amazing* and *staying amazing*, that makes the truly great companies *great*.

This Book Is for You

I wrote this book for *everyone* who has the job of keeping customers happy. That means you can use this book to make the journey to *amazement* regardless of whether you are

- A frontline employee who has lots of direct contact with customers
- A behind-the-scenes employee who has little or no direct contact with customers
- A manager or team leader
- A CEO, owner, or founder of a company
- Or a solo entrepreneur

Finally . . .

I want to hear from you. Any feedback about the book would be greatly appreciated. And please, send me your stories. I would love to hear about the companies you admire and, most important, *your* company. Are you already operating at the level we call the *cult of amazement?* Or did you have to work up to that level? As I write my newsletters, blogs, and books, it would be great to include your stories.

Please drop me a line:

Shep Hyken, CSP, CPAE

shep@hyken.com
www.hyken.com
www.CultOfTheCustomer.com

Part One

THE PURPOSE OF YOUR BUSINESS

Chapter One

THE GENIE AND THE ICE CREAM SHOP

nce upon a time, a genie paid a visit to the town square of Businessland, where he met three entrepreneurs, each of whom wanted to open an ice cream stand.

"I will grant each of you one wish—give you anything you ask of me—if, and only if, granting your wish will *truly* ensure the success of your venture," the genie promised. As he floated sedately on an orange puff of smoke poised about three feet above the center of the town square, the genie stared ominously at the three entrepreneurs. "Speak your wish," he said, pointing at the first entrepreneur, "and speak well."

The first entrepreneur thought for a moment and then said: "My wish is the best possible ice cream to sell here in Businessland—the most delicious ice cream on earth."

"I shall not grant it," said the genie with a frown. "The best ice cream on earth would not guarantee your success."

He turned to the second entrepreneur. "Speak your wish—and speak well."

The response came quickly: "My wish is that you should grant me the very best location in Businessland, in a place where my ice cream shop will be noticed by all who pass through the city."

"I shall not grant it," said the genie, frowning again. "The best location on earth would not guarantee your success."

The genie cast a doubtful eye on the third entrepreneur, saying: "Yours is the last wish. Speak it—and speak well."

The third entrepreneur smiled confidently. "I have ice cream," she said, "though it may not be the best on earth, and I have a storefront in mind, although it may not be the best location. My wish," she continued in a firm voice, "is that I should have a never-ending supply of *loyal customers* lined up outside the door of my ice cream shop every day."

The genie grinned broadly.

"You have spoken well," the genie said. "Your wish is my command." With that, he cast his spell, and from that moment on, the third entrepreneur's business thrived (much to the chagrin of the first two).

Without customers, it doesn't matter how good the ice cream is.

Without customers, it doesn't matter where you put the ice cream shop.

Without customers, you don't have a business.

Now, I may not be a genie, and I can't grant you any wishes. But what I *can* do is give you the tools and information you need to deliver a customer experience that creates *loyal* customers—the kind of customers who not only keep coming back for more ice cream but also refer their friends and associates to your ice cream stand—or whatever your business is.

If you're interested in finding out what will help you transform *customers* into *evangelists* . . . read on.

Chapter Two

DO YOU NEED THIS BOOK?

You need this book if your world revolves around customers. And if you're like most of us, that's exactly the group around whom your world *does* revolve, because customers make business happen. Customers make it possible for us to switch on our lights, pay our employees and our bills, and develop new products and services—essentially, grow our businesses. In the end, customers make it possible for our organizations to exist.

Customers are to businesses what air is to human beings. They are essential for survival yet easy to take for granted. Customers make it possible for us to continue with our business and its purpose. So ask yourself:

What is the purpose of your business?

When I ask people that question at the outset of my speeches, workshops, and seminars, I usually get some variation of "Make money, make a profit."

That's a *goal*, however, and if you confuse your purpose with your goal, you run the risk of never reaching your goal. Making money and turning a profit are not the *purpose* of your business. Harvard Business School Professor Theodore Levitt writes in his book *The Marketing Imagination*, "The purpose of every business and organization is to *get and keep* customers."[1]

No matter what you do—and regardless of whether you work for yourself or as part of a larger organization—*you depend on your customers for a living*. If you hope to succeed in any meaningful sense of that word, you *must* understand your customers and appreciate what they want. Without customers, your operation is dead. If you fail to satisfy your customers, they will buy from the competition or maybe simply stop buying.

By the way, *customers* can be clients, guests, patrons, patients, members, buyers, readers, subscribers—and any number of other sorts of people. Throughout this book, I will be using the word *customer* to generically define anyone with whom you do business—anyone who pays you or your organization for any product or service. And I will use the words *internal customer* to describe people with whom you work and who may, at any time, be dependent on you or your department.

You need this book if . . .

- . . . you are on the front line, dealing with customers.
- . . . you manage people who are on the front line, dealing with customers.
- . . . you lead an organization, department, or small business that has any employees who are on the front line, dealing with customers.
- . . . you created an organization, or have a company, that has automated processes your customers interact with—even if those interactions don't involve face-to-face or voice-to-voice contact—such as e-mail, voice mail, web sites, or blogs.

. . . you lead an already *amazing* company that wants to *stay amazing*—or you want to become even more *amazing* to your customers.

Big and small companies alike rely on customers. Organizations with lots of employees—and those with hardly any—rely on customers. Once a customer experiences any aspect of your business—in person, on the phone, or over the Internet—you need this book. That's because all of these customers upon whom you and your company rely for business will make their decisions based not simply on customer service—but on the overall *customer experience* as well.

The customer experience comes in part from service, but in the larger sense it is everything created by any and all contact with your operation. Your goal is to improve the quality of the customer experience.

Improving the quality of the customer experience requires doing more than putting up posters claiming "The Customer Is Number One." That may (or may not) improve the décor of the employee lounge, but if that's all you do, it's unlikely to have any impact on what customers actually experience.

Improving the quality of your customers' experience requires your organization to create genuine relationships with both its *internal* and *external* customers. You'll see why this idea of connecting with internal *and* external customers is so important in just a moment. For now, though, let me ask you this: Would you say that you have *satisfied* customers?

If you said or thought yes—even for a moment—and felt good about that answer, turn the page.

If you're like most of the clients I work with, you probably thought or said, "Yes—my customers are pretty satisfied."

In that case, you definitely need this book because satisfying your customer is not enough.

In today's environment, simply satisfying customers can put you at risk for going out of business.

By the Numbers

Between 60 percent and 80 percent of customers who describe themselves as satisfied do not go back to do more business with the company they're satisfied with.[2]

You must build experiences that create not merely satisfied but *loyal* customers—customers who not only return to do business with you but also sing your praises and act as advocates on your behalf.

For our purposes in this book, the concept of loyalty represents *more* than repeat business from an individual buyer. It signifies an opportunity to market with incredible effectiveness and cost-efficiency. Your truly loyal customers will not only buy from you but also do much of your selling for you. *They will become your advocates!* This book shows you how to create the experiences that build that kind of loyalty.

What Is the Cult of the Customer?

The cult of the customer is a way of looking at experiences and relationships. It is a strategy for consistently delivering not just satisfaction but *amazement*.

The cult of the customer is a method of operating, working, and living that is focused on the consistent delivery of experiences that I call Moments of Magic®. Moments of Magic are the *positive touch points* that your company and your employees have with customers. There are as many possible touch points as there are customers, and they can come in many different forms—person to person, voice to voice, over the Internet, or even via text message. These Moments of Magic are vitally important for both internal and external customers!

A Moment of Magic is simply an above-average experience.

Sometimes it's a little bit better than average or satisfactory. Sometimes it's a wow moment or an example of someone truly going the extra mile. An individual Moment of Magic may not inspire *amazement* in and of itself, but a *sequence* of such moments *will* inspire *amazement*!

Amazement Is a Central Experience within the Cult of the Customer

It takes time and effort to create these consistent experiences and make your way into the cult of the customer, but it's definitely worth the trouble, because the rewards are exponentially higher than any investment you make along the way. Only *amazement* delivers the legions of unpaid, passionate advocates for your organization that I refer to as the army of evangelists.

Make no mistake: These evangelists are not merely *satisfied.* They are *amazed! That's a customer on a whole different level.* Most of us, unfortunately, are aiming too low when we aspire to satisfaction. And we usually don't even know we're shooting too low, which is a shame.

By the Numbers

Stock prices can be positively affected by loyalty. As an example, a recent study by Walker Information for the wireless communications industry indicated that over a three year period, the "loyalty leaders" in the industry outperformed the "loyalty laggards" by 173%![3]

Why Use the Word *Cult*?

Some people might consider *cult* to be a bad word. Although some of the most visible cults of modern times are religious or fanatical and sometimes outside the norm, a cult is simply a shared system of belief, experience, or interest. It's part of being human. A group of people who share a deeper than usual passion for a hobby, sport, or type of music can be considered a cult. It is really nothing more than an extreme passion, and in this case, the passion is business and customers. Think of the word *cult* as being part of the word *culture*. The culture we want in our business is a cultlike devotion to creating an *amazing* experience that will turn satisfied customers into evangelists. That is what this book is about—*The Cult of the Customer*.

You are already part of some kind of cult that connects to your customer, but which cult do you belong to right now? I've already told you about the cult I refer to as the cult of the customer. Here's another way to think about the very same system of belief and experience: *the cult of amazement*.

As its name suggests, the cult is dedicated to delivering *amazement*. Remember, this is not necessarily the result of perfect customer service (as in never screwing up) but instead the result of making Moments of Magic part of a consistent, ongoing *pattern* of experiences. Remember, these are experiences that are simply *above average*, which the customer comes to expect and rely on.

In short, we are creating customer confidence and extraordinary loyalty by creating a consistently above-average customer experience. The key word here is *consistency*.

There is no loyalty without confidence, and there is no confidence without consistency!

Now consider this:

Amazement is the result of a consistent sequence of Moments of Magic . . . for both our customers *and* the people who interact with our customers.

Delivering these moments, *both internally and externally,* is the most important task any organization faces. Why? Because, as Ted Levitt points out, the purpose of every business—of every organization—is to get and *keep* customers!

The Five Cults

We'll be talking in much greater detail about the five cults later on, but take a look at these brief descriptions now, and ask yourself which best describes *your customer's* orientation to you and your operation.

The Cult of Uncertainty

- The customer says, "What's going to happen?"
- There is no consistency. Customers simply aren't sure what's going to happen. Some of the customers within this cult know little or nothing about your business, because they haven't done business with you before.
- Some customers may have experienced inconsistencies when they did business with you in the past.
- The cult of uncertainty is by far the largest cult and has many subdivisions. Service in this cult runs the gamut from unacceptable to average or satisfactory. *It is not consistent.* Despite occasional signs of excellent service, the experience typically is average at best.

- Some of the customers within this cult may actually be satisfied.
- Customers in this cult offer *no real loyalty* to your business.

The Cult of Alignment

- The customer says, "Okay, I hear what you're promising. Prove it to me."
- The customer is aware of your brand promise and value proposition, which creates at least some *curiosity* about whether the experience will match the promise. Notice that the customer is not simply uncertain—as in the previous cult—but has a specific expectation.
- Even though customers know the promise, they have yet to experience it. They want proof.

The Cult of Experience

- The customer says, "I had a good experience. What will happen the next time?"
- This is where you begin to win what advertising and marketing people call top-of-mind awareness *for the actual experience,* not just the brand.
- Even after enjoying a good experience, the customer is still not loyal, even though he or she may be satisfied. It takes *multiple* positive experiences to get customers to the next cult.

The Cult of Ownership

- The customer says, "Wow. I had *another* great experience, and *another* one! There's a pattern here. I like this company. This is where I want to be!"
- This is where the customer starts to lean into your organization. This is the first sign of customer confidence and loyalty.

- You begin to deliver a pattern of *consistent above-average experiences* to the customer.
- With the consistency of above-average experiences, something remarkable happens. The customer joins the fifth and highest cult—*the cult of amazement.*

The Cult of Amazement

- The customer becomes an *evangelist* and says to friends and associates, "This company is great! You've got to try this!"
- Ownership matures into actual loyalty.
- The customer's expectations are high, and they are consistently met, if not exceeded. This creates confidence, which can lead to loyalty.
- Repeat business is likely. Recommendations and referrals naturally follow *amazement.*

You've almost certainly experienced the *cult of amazement* firsthand, as a customer. Start by remembering any company you enthusiastically recommended or praised. What consistent experiences brought you to that point?

Consider a time when you experienced great service at a superb restaurant or at a hotel where the staff was completely attuned to your every need. Or perhaps you encountered a vendor who went above and beyond the call of duty for you. Then, when you had the chance to recommend the restaurant, hotel, or business to a friend, you enthusiastically did so. In all likelihood, it wasn't a single *moment* that turned you into an evangelist. It was the business's ability to deliver multiple Moments of Magic to you *on a regular basis* that transformed you into an advocate—an evangelist—for the company.

Only when customers are *routinely* impressed by the experience they receive do they join the *cult of amazement* and start recommending the experience to others.

Inside the Organization

What we may not recognize is that before any organization *can deliver amazement* on a consistent basis *externally*, it must endure certain predictable phases. The employees themselves must make their own way into the *cult of amazement before* they can consistently deliver the experience to their customers.

This is how the same progression plays out on the employee side.

The Cult of Uncertainty

- Employees say, "We aren't sure."
- Employees have not been trained properly—or at all.
- Employees may not know what's coming next.
- Employees simply may not have access to what they need to be successful.

The Cult of Alignment

- Employees say, "Okay, I understand what we're promising. Prove it to me, so I can prove it to the customer."
- Employees understand the brand promise and the value proposition; they understand what your organization is trying to do.
- Employees have been properly trained.
- Employees have not, however, personally delivered *consistently* above-average experiences to customers.

The Cult of Experience

- Employees say, "Wow, it works. I delivered a Moment of Magic. I created a great experience."
- Employees want to repeat what they've done with the customer. At this stage, they are starting to get positive feedback.
- Employees enjoy emotional satisfaction from their success.
- Employees begin to experience the organization's brand promise for themselves—as if they were the customers.
- The transition between *uncertainty* and *alignment* is the most critical for the customer-focused organization.

The Cult of Ownership

- Employees say, "This is getting to be a habit! Great experiences are becoming routine! There's a pattern emerging! It works and I'm focused. I know what to do. This is where I belong!"
- Employees start implementing a process and fine-tune that process.
- Employees *routinely* experience the organization's brand promise as if they were the customer. When employees themselves are treated this way, they have a model they can use for creating positive customer experiences.
- Employees have an emotional connection to the organization.

The Cult of Amazement

- Employees become *evangelists* for their own company; they get addicted to delivering *amazement* and say, "I love working here!"
- Employees become deeply invested in a shared system of belief that puts the customer experience first.
- Employees are not just going to work each day but integrating what they do as a part of their social identity.

- Employees are fully present and engaged for their customers.
- Employees, like the customers they serve, are loyal to their organization.

The *cult of amazement* is the highest possible cult of the customer. It's where we all want to be. This book shows how to build such a cult—or, if you prefer, such a culture.

Every organization that deals with customers operates within one of the five clearly definable customer cults. Unfortunately, most are operating at a level that does not consistently result in *amazement.*

If you want to create a great experience, achieve loyalty, and develop an army of evangelists, your customers must experience— and you must operate within—*the cult of amazement.* Some of us are already there, but for most of us, getting to the *cult of amazement* means *working our way up* through the other four cults.

This takes effort and persistence. Let me emphasize once again: Creating a *cult of amazement* doesn't mean you have to be *amazing* all of the time! Very often, it just means being *better* than average *most* of the time, with occasional bursts of truly superior service.

Overall, it is the consistent delivery of little things that brings customers into the *cult of amazement.*

Is This Going to Be Hard to Understand?

No. The cult of the customer is quite easy to understand. But like anything worth attaining, it takes effort.

The cult of the customer is not some far-flung, hard-to-grasp academic concept. If you have ever recommended a company or service to someone else, the *cult of amazement* is *already* on display in your own world and in your own choices as a consumer or as a businessperson.

The *cult of amazement* may be waiting for you the next time you hail a cab, purchase a new computer for your company, check into a hotel, or buy a pair of shoes. It's possible anytime you do business with anyone.

Keep reading, and I'll show you exactly what I mean.

The Keepers

- The purpose of your business is not to make money; that is a goal. The purpose is to get and keep customers. (Dr. Theodore Levitt)
- Satisfying your customers is not enough. Satisfied customers are not loyal customers.
- It is the total customer experience—not just customer service—that creates customer loyalty.
- There are five customer cults. The highest level is the *cult of amazement,* where the customer becomes an *evangelist* for our organization.
- The *cult of amazement* results when we *consistently* deliver Moments of Magic—that is, habitually provide a series of (at least) above-average customer experiences.
- To move up the ladder to the *cult of amazement,* we must engage not only our customers but everyone in our organization—including our internal customers who may never actually meet or speak with outside customers.
- There is no loyalty without confidence, and there is no confidence without consistency!

Chapter Three

THE THREE FORCES

One of the questions people ask me about the *cult of amazement* is "How many people does it take to get it started?"

The answer is actually pretty simple: one. Whether you are a solo entrepreneur, an employee inside a larger organization, or the CEO of a Fortune 100 company, this is a revolution you can start on your own. This chapter introduces and explains the three kinds of service forces that enable you to launch this movement, regardless of the size of your organization.

The Three Service Forces

There are three kinds of service forces that can deliver the *cult of amazement:*

- You can join the *force of one,* meaning that you operate at the *cult of amazement* as a solo entrepreneur.
- You can join the *force within,* meaning that you personally operate at the *cult of amazement* as part of a larger group *of any*

size that is currently stuck in one of the other cults (most likely the uncertainty cult).

- You can join the *force of many*, meaning that *everyone* in your organization is operating under the *cult of amazement.*

These are the three forces by which your customers can experience *amazement* and become evangelists for your organization. *Evangelists not only stick around; they also seek to expand the cult and refer new customers to your organization.* When customers aren't *amazed,* they're much less likely to forgive unacceptable levels of customer service from someone in your organization and, thus, more likely to leave you for your competition.

By the Numbers

A recent study of 1,000 consumers by global management consulting company Accenture cited subpar customer service as the primary reason consumers leave product or service providers—despite massive investment in customer relationship management (CRM) technologies in recent years. Fully half of the customers surveyed by Accenture identified poor customer service as the reason for their decision to change service providers over the past 12 months; two-thirds of consumers reported no personal perception of improvement in customer service levels over a period of *five years.*[1]

The Force of One

If you're familiar with my books *Moments of Magic*® and *The Loyal Customer,* you'll recognize the following story. It warrants repetition, because it's the ultimate example of a force of one.

Frank the Cabdriver

I'd just given a presentation in Dallas on a sweltering, 102-degree day. I was sweaty, exhausted, and looking forward to getting home to St. Louis. Frank saw me walking out of the convention center. He pulled up to the curb and stepped out of the cab to help me with my bags. He was wearing cut-off shorts and a T-shirt, had messed-up hair, and looked like he hadn't shaved in a week. With some hesitation, I handed him my bags and started to get into the cab. I thought, "Look at him. What is the inside of this cab going to be like?"

Once inside the cab, however, I was reminded that appearances can be deceiving.

The air-conditioning was on, which was a relief. I realized I had gone from over-the-top, near-heat-stroke conditions outside to a refreshing, downright cool temperature inside the vehicle. Once I settled in, I noticed that the cab was not just clean—it was meticulously tidy. On the seat were two neatly folded newspapers; on the hump that divided the two rear seats sat a bucket of ice and two soft drinks. I was astonished.

Eventually, Frank got in the cab, picked up a plate of candy from the front seat, and offered me a piece. He said, "Make yourself at home. Are you in a hurry for your flight, or is it okay if I do the speed limit?"

I couldn't remember the last time a cabdriver asked me a question like that. I was pretty sure it had never happened to me before.

"Take your time," I said, settling back to read the paper and drink a soda. I had three hours before my flight took off, and suddenly I wasn't in such a rush to get to the airport.

A few minutes later, Frank asked if I'd ever seen the famous fountain at Las Colinas. He explained that Las Colinas is a business community on the way to the airport and that the fountain featured statues of beautiful life-size horses running across water. He explained that it was just off the highway and the most beautiful fountain in the Dallas area—maybe in the entire

United States! He went on to say that if I had a few extra minutes, then he would love to show it to me—at no extra charge. I agreed and said, "Show me the fountain!" I remember wondering: "What am I getting here—a cab ride or a VIP tour of the city?"

So Frank showed me the fountain. We actually got out of the cab, and he explained the history behind the fountain and the artist who created it. When we got back in the cab, we exchanged business cards. Before he dropped me off at the airport, he said, "The next time you come back to Dallas, give me a call a day or two ahead of time. Let me know what time you're coming in, what airline and flight number you're on, and I'll pick you up. I'll treat you the same as a limousine driver would, but I'll charge you the same flat cabdriver rate. I'll even park the car outside, come inside, and meet you at the baggage claim area. When you walk over to get your bags, I'll be standing there, ready to help you. Don't worry, you'll recognize me."

I certainly would! When he dropped me off at the airport, I gave Frank a nice tip. He said, "Thank you, and I hope to see you the next time you're in Dallas." I promised him he would see me—and I meant it!

Four days later, I was in my office in St. Louis, going through the day's mail—*and there was a thank-you note from Frank, my cabdriver in Dallas!*

Until Frank retired, who do you think I called whenever I went back to Dallas? Who do you think I recommended to other people when they needed a cab in Dallas?

Frank was operating in the *cult of amazement,* as a force of one—and an *amazing* force, at that.

The Force Within

Most airlines have not enjoyed a stellar reputation for customer service in recent years. It's not my style to criticize individual companies, though, so I'm calling the carrier in this story Anonymous Airlines.

I walked up to the gate agent of Anonymous Airlines, very upset. My flight to Los Angeles had just been canceled, and I wanted to know why. The agent, a poised, smiling man in his mid-thirties named Harold, heard me out and then asked me if I knew why the flight had been canceled. I said, "No."

Harold apologized for the problem and explained that the plane had been found to have bad brakes. He didn't make excuses; he gave me an explanation. He then asked, "You don't want to be on that airplane when it lands with bad brakes, do you?"

I responded, "No."

"That's right!" Harold said, smiling. "You do want to get to Los Angeles as close to on time as possible, don't you?"

I answered, "Yes!"

Harold asked where I wanted to go in Los Angeles, and I told him downtown. He mentioned that the Los Angeles International Airport was just one of four airports serving the metro area. He suggested that I take a flight to Burbank that left 10 minutes earlier. "By arriving ten minutes early," he explained, "you'll make up the extra time it takes to get downtown." He smiled, handed me my ticket, and asked if there was anything else he could help me with. I thanked him and walked away a happy customer.

Harold had given me answers. He had taken care of my problem. He had treated me with respect. He had a great attitude. Harold was operating as part of a *force within*. Many of Harold's fellow employees and managers didn't treat customers so well. Even though Anonymous Airlines was operating in the cult of uncertainty, that didn't stop Harold from making sure that his personal zone of influence was operating under the *cult of amazement*—and providing a truly satisfying experience for his customers.

The Force of Many

Once in a while, I'm fortunate enough to stay at the Ritz-Carlton, a superb chain of luxury hotels. During one of my stays on a business trip, I mentioned to the hotel manager that I was getting married. The manager said, "Mr. Hyken, why don't you stay at our St. Louis Ritz on your wedding night?"

That seemed like a great idea to me—and what a pleasant surprise it was for my fiancée. When I surprised her with the idea, she thought I was the most romantic guy on earth!

The big day rolled around. I checked in that afternoon, before the ceremony. Our room wasn't ready, so I checked the bags with the bellhop, who told me that the bags would be waiting for us in our room when we came back that night.

That evening, after the wedding, when my wife and I stepped through the main door of the hotel, the doorman—a complete stranger to both of us—greeted us enthusiastically: "Welcome, Mr. and Mrs. Hyken!"

You can't imagine the kind of impression that welcome left! My wife told me that it was the first time that anyone except in the wedding itself had addressed her as "Mrs. Hyken." The rest of the staff was equally *amazing*. They gave us the royal treatment. The service was great, and our room was magnificent.

There was just one problem: Our bags weren't in the room. And when we called down to the front desk to ask about them, it quickly became apparent that the bags had been lost.

Operating within the *cult of amazement* doesn't mean you are perfect and never make mistakes. What it means is that you're much better positioned than anyone else to recover from a mistake. And the employees at the Ritz-Carlton were about to prove that.

I went downstairs to talk to the staff at the front desk. I told them that our luggage was lost, that we had no toiletries, and that the only clothes we had were my tuxedo and my wife's wedding dress.

The man at the front desk knew that it was our wedding night—I believe everyone on staff must have known—and he picked up the telephone and dialed a number. I heard him say to the person on the phone, "Mr. Hyken is here in front of us. We don't have his bags. *Tonight, we have an opportunity.*"

Once the opportunity was discovered, the Ritz employees moved quickly into *service recovery* mode. First and foremost, the staff apologized for the inconvenience and promised me that they were going to turn the hotel upside down to locate our bags. In the interim, would we please accept, with their compliments, anything that seemed appropriate from the hotel gift shop? It was closed, but of course they would open it so that we could get what we needed.

We walked away with sweatshirts, gym shorts, toothbrushes, toothpaste—anything our hearts desired. The Ritz employees were doing whatever they could to take care of us and manage the so-called opportunity.

The next morning, we got a message from the front desk that the staff had located our bags. *Amazingly,* they had made their way into the lost and found. When we finally went downstairs to check out, the staff apologized again for the inconvenience and talked to us to make sure that we were happy.

At some hotels and hotel chains, losing the bags of a bride and groom on their honeymoon night would create a Moment of Misery™: a negative impression that could ruin the experience. In this case, the Ritz-Carlton took that same event and, through flawless execution, turned a Moment of Misery into a Moment of Magic. They were quick to respond—and with an excellent attitude. The way they managed this opportunity restored my confidence and turned me into a Ritz-Carlton evangelist— someone who was really eager to sing the praises of the establishment to others.

The staff of the Ritz-Carlton was operating within the *cult of amazement* as a *force of many.* The guiding culture of that entire hotel, and indeed the entire chain, is one of sheer *amazement.* It's not surprising to me that the Ritz-Carlton does a great job of winning repeat business from its customers and turning its clients into evangelists.

By the Numbers

Establishing a *cult of amazement* helps you do a better job of retaining customers, and retaining customers makes sound business sense. The cost of retaining an existing customer is estimated at a fifth to a sixth of the cost of attracting a brand new one.[2]

Please understand that you do not need to be the CEO of the company to make the journey to *amazement,* although, as you will see, CEOs certainly have built entire companies around the principles of the *cult of amazement* and achieved significant long-term competitive advantages as a result. But even if your CEO decides this is not a priority, *you* can make the *cult of amazement* a priority. Nor do you need to be the manager of your department to make the journey to *amazement.* Although managers can lead, and have led, their teams on this journey, you can be a *force within,* make the journey yourself, and take your colleagues with you along the way.

The Keepers

- You can operate in three possible *service forces* at the *cult of amazement.*
- When you operate as a *force of one,* you personally exemplify the *cult of amazement* in your relationship with the customer, typically as a solo entrepreneur.
- When you operate as part of the *force within,* you personally exemplify the *cult of amazement* within a larger enterprise that

is, as a whole, stuck at some other phase, typically the uncertainty stage.

- When you operate as part of the *force of many*, you are functioning as part of an enterprise that is, as a whole, operating in the *cult of amazement.*
- Customers in the *cult of amazement* act as evangelists for your enterprise. Evangelists not only stick around—they seek to expand the cult by looking for new customers for your organization.
- When customers aren't *amazed,* they're more likely to be unforgiving when they receive unacceptable levels of customer service from someone in your organization, and thus they are more likely to leave you for the competition!

Part Two

THE FIVE CULTS

Chapter Four

UNCERTAINTY

onsider this: You are *already* a member of a cult that reflects both your customer's reality *and* your organization's reality. You are either standing *still* in the cult of uncertainty or in *motion* toward a new standard. The standard at the top of the continuum is *amazement.* (See Figure 4.1.)

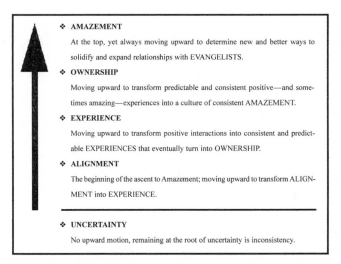

❖ **AMAZEMENT**

At the top, yet always moving upward to determine new and better ways to solidify and expand relationships with EVANGELISTS.

❖ **OWNERSHIP**

Moving upward to transform predictable and consistent positive—and sometimes amazing—experiences into a culture of consistent AMAZEMENT.

❖ **EXPERIENCE**

Moving upward to transform positive interactions into consistent and predictable EXPERIENCES that eventually turn into OWNERSHIP.

❖ **ALIGNMENT**

The beginning of the ascent to Amazement; moving upward to transform ALIGNMENT into EXPERIENCE.

❖ **UNCERTAINTY**

No upward motion, remaining at the root of uncertainty is inconsistency.

Figure 4.1   The Five Cults

The lowest stage, uncertainty, is static; there is virtually no upward motion, and any movement is eroded with inconsistency. This is the point from which most companies operate. *Though many customers are satisfied at the level of uncertainty, most are not loyal to your organization.* This area is the easiest place to settle into a sense of complacency and miss clues that there's a problem with customers or employees.

The Way We Do Business

The cult of uncertainty is inconsistent and potentially alienating for both customers and employees; it is unfortunately also the way that most companies do business. We have gotten used to it, but it does not deliver *consistently above-average experiences.*

It's sad but true that most of us spend a whole lot of time—as both customers and employees—in the cult of uncertainty, where customers *do not know* what level of service they're about to receive and may even expect the worst. It is the cult where employees may not have the tools and/or training necessary to deliver consistently above-average experiences for their internal and external customers.

Although the transition out of uncertainty seems simple in theory, it takes organizations a great deal of time and energy to move out of this stage and into the next level: the cult of alignment. The transition is a little like the beginning of a roller-coaster ride. An immense amount of energy is expended to get to the top of the first hill. Once the roller coaster goes over the top, gravity and momentum take over, and the real ride begins. Similarly, once you have left the cult of uncertainty and make it into the cult of alignment, you've made a major breakthrough. It's an easier journey from that point forward. But getting up that hill takes work!

In the cult of uncertainty, you don't yet have a consistent process; even worse, you haven't yet engaged with any guiding vision or purpose for the customer. That's what keeps the roller coaster from making it over the top of the first hill. When you are operating within this realm, you may deliver good service, bad service, indifferent service, or even, on occasion, great service. But you won't be delivering above-average service *consistently*, and that means the customer is having unreliable experiences.

By the Numbers

A recent survey about online purchases found a direct correlation between the overall *experience* of consumers and the loyalty of those consumers to online sellers. The same report found that 80 percent of online sellers surveyed believed that "improving the usability, usefulness, and enjoyability" of the online experience was a bigger priority for them than it was in years past. In other words, the priority is the *customer experience.*[1]

The question to ask yourself is "What does your customer *consistently* experience?" No matter how many people may be operating at the *cult of amazement* in your company, if there is a lack of consistency or a lack of process, *your organization is always at the mercy of its weakest link.* And sometimes the weakest link is the person at the top of the organization.

Meet Mike Hardhead

Mike Hardhead is the founder and CEO of WidgetBlue, a manufacturer of widgets. One week ago, Mike was attending a big industry trade show when he got a high-priority message on his Blackberry: *BigCo has canceled its fall order, says it now has a contract with National Widget.* This was bad, bad news, and it was going to put a big hole in yearly earnings. And to lose a long-term client like BigCo to National Widget! Mike wanted to get back to his booth as soon as possible and grill his sales manager. But as he turned the corner, he caught sight of a short, kindly man in his mid-seventies with a lean, wrinkled face. It was Harlan Love, the CEO of his rival company, National Widget.

Love saw Mike and walked across the busy aisle of the convention toward him. Mike forced a smile and shook the old man's tiny hand obediently. Harlan Love had given Mike his first chance in the industry by selecting him for an internship, back when he was in college.

"How have you been, Mike?" the old man asked. "It's been a while."

"Very well, Mr. Love," Mike replied. "Very well. Busy, though. I'm up to my eyeballs in orders."

Mr. Love smiled patiently and nodded his head.

"I hope you can make it by our booth," Mike said. "We're number 643. Got a meeting coming up," Mike lied. "I'd stay longer to chat, but . . . "

"Of course," said Mr. Love. "We'll catch up later."

Mike shook the small man's weathered hand once again, caught the gentle gaze of his former mentor a second time, turned briskly, and started walking away. He couldn't wait to get his sales manager in front of him. Losing the BigCo account! And to Harlan Love, of all people!

Before Mike could get too far from Mr. Love, he heard, "Mike, I want you to know that I didn't steal your account. BigCo came to us."

Mike stopped and turned—then stared at the old man.

"That's right. Your biggest customer came to us. If you waste your time being angry at your sales manager, you're going to miss out on what's really happening. The problem is that BigCo was simply *satisfied*. In fact, most of your customers are satisfied, but they're not loyal. If you're wondering how to head off problems with any of your other customers, you should start by looking *inside* first. I hope you aren't upset, but I thought you needed to know."

There was a long pause.

"Start by looking inside," Mike repeated. "Thanks, Mr. Love. I'll do that."

"Our Customers Are Pretty Happy"

Mike didn't realize that his company was operating at the cult of uncertainty. His customers seemed all right. His company was profitable. He never would have thought there were any problems. Yet his company was indeed vulnerable—he had just lost one of his biggest customers.

Whenever Mike walked through his call center and talked to his salespeople, all he heard about were satisfied customers. He figured there had to be a process in place somewhere, because the customers all seemed satisfied. Indeed, they were satisfied—most of them, at any rate. They weren't *delighted.* Yet, as Mike's old mentor pointed out, there was a problem. There seemed to be a problem in consistently delivering an above-average customer experience. And Mr. Love had said to start looking on the inside.

Mike's customers had no loyalty to his company, even though they were technically satisfied with the service they received from WidgetBlue. The company was highly vulnerable to challenges from competitors. How had he let things get to this point?

By the Numbers

Two-thirds of customers do not feel valued by those serving them. In other words, the company is not showing any loyalty toward the customer, so why should the customer show loyalty toward the company?[2]

If customers had problems, it's unlikely that Mike ever heard about them. Most companies operating at the cult of uncertainty do not have effective communication channels set up for their customers. As a result, people on the front line at WidgetBlue encountered only a small fraction of the complaints that actually needed resolving. And of course, WidgetBlue employees did not seek out problems.

By the Numbers

It's estimated that only 10 percent of customer complaints are ever articulated.[3]

Only happy stories made their way up to Mike's office because he had instilled a culture of *don't get caught* at WidgetBlue. Whenever there was a problem with a widget installation, a delivery, or a misplaced order, the people at WidgetBlue would usually get yelled at instead of being coached on how to improve the situation and ensure that it wouldn't recur in the future. This pattern played out from the top on down. It's how Mike treated his managers, and it's how his managers treated the people on the front line and, for that matter, everyone else in the organization. The process that had emerged was an *error-avoidance* process, not a *customer experience* process. People didn't want to get screamed at, so they didn't admit that there ever was—or ever could be—a problem with a customer. And they certainly didn't go out on a limb to identify or solve a customer's problem in a creative, previously unimagined way. That might be a mistake, and mistakes meant that the hammer would come down!

Mike had misplaced his hiring and training priorities. WidgetBlue started out as a tough little technology-driven company that was willing to stake its reputation on the quality of its products. The company was creative and loved to take on the difficult projects their customers brought to them. The quality and design of the products that WidgetBlue shipped were still high, and Mike's people got more than enough technical training on the ins and outs of industrial widgets. However, they lacked soft skills training—the kind of training that gives employees the skills they need to create a great customer interaction. What's worse, WidgetBlue had a lot of people on the front line who really shouldn't have been there, as well as a lot of people working internally who could be helping to make things better on the front line for his customers. Things were mixed up, but Mike didn't realize that yet.

In part, that's because Mike's standards were too low. Like any capable CEO, Mike called his company's customers from time to time, and he learned that most of them were, in fact, pretty satisfied with what WidgetBlue had given them. Mike heard generally positive product feedback from his customers, and he felt pretty good about it. What he heard confirmed what he believed about his widgets, which is that they were of very high quality, and indeed, they were. The problem was that Mike didn't realize that this standard of satisfaction was too low to give his company any meaningful competitive advantage in the long term. In addition, Mike was not asking his customers the right questions; the ones he was posing were simply too general. Questions like ''So how are we doing?'' or ''Did you get everything you ordered?'' weren't specific enough. On top of that, Mike had not yet realized that satisfaction does not equal loyalty in the widget industry, or anywhere else.

What Does Mike's Cult Say Is Happening?

Remember, a cult is *a shared system of belief and experience.* Mike's current cult was saying that things are working pretty well at Widgetblue. Mike had gotten used to and comfortable with his existing system of belief and experience. That's another way of saying that the cult within which he was operating—the cult of uncertainty—was now reinforcing itself, which this cult is very good at doing. In essence, Mike was saying to himself, ''This is the way we do business here.''

As a result, moving out of uncertainty and into alignment will take some concentrated effort from everyone at WidgetBlue. The first and perhaps most important element of that effort is recognizing where WidgetBlue actually was at the moment that they decided to change—and that was a part of the cult of uncertainty. Such a process of self-examination is not always easy or pleasant. But once Mike realized where his company actually was and what it was actually doing, he could decide that it was time to start the journey out of uncertainty. Once he committed to that journey, he found that the other four cults follow in sequence fairly quickly.

The Cult of Uncertainty Can Take Many Forms

This story is just one example of a company operating under uncertainty. Your company may be facing very different circumstances. Remember that although you may be working in what is thought of as a good company, and although your customers may be saying they are satisfied, that does not mean you are out of uncertainty. Many of the symptoms in this phase seem benign. The experiences you deliver to your customers may be good, but are they good enough to protect you from a competitor? (See Figure 4.2.)

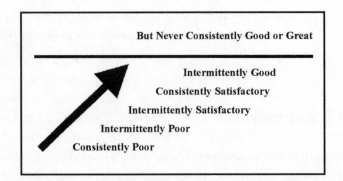

Figure 4.2   Uncertainty Service Continuum Graphic

The first step toward moving beyond the uncertainty phase is acknowledging that you are in it!

Case Study: Terry Black's Super Smokers BBQ

Terry Black's Super Smokers BBQ is the best barbecue restaurant in St. Louis, Missouri, and famous for its award-winning food. When the restaurant won a contract to supply a major sports stadium with barbecue concessions, Terry thought he had made a significant competitive breakthrough.

But it wasn't long into the venture that Terry sampled the food served at the stadium and realized something was wrong. There was inconsistency. Some of the corn on the cob was overcooked. Some of the meats were dried out. Terry had found his way into the cult of uncertainty. Thousands of potential restaurant customers were getting a substandard product that he would never tolerate at his restaurant, and his current restaurant customers were not getting a stadium product that was consistent with their previous experiences.

Terry immediately realized his problem and decided to revise his remote game plan to offer fewer food items and provide better employee training at the stadium location. His revised plan enabled him to provide a stadium experience that was similar to the dining experience customers would get at the restaurant. The sacrifice of giving up variety to maintain quality was a smart move. The stadium venture not only became profitable but also became a powerful magnet that drew people to his main restaurant and catering business.

What Is Uncertainty?

Uncertainty is inconsistency. It can come from lacking a process for delivering a consistently positive customer experience. It's what was plaguing WidgetBlue, and what will continue to plague

WidgetBlue—until Mike figures out what's working best on the front line and gets it to work consistently across the organization, just as Terry Black's Super Smokers BBQ restaurant did.

What would Mike—or anyone else at WidgetBlue—have to do to move the process along as quickly as possible? A good start would be to check the following list.

Symptoms That Your Company Is Currently Operating in the Cult of Uncertainty

The symptoms I hear from people and organizations that are operating in the cult of uncertainty sound like this:

- Service is inconsistent.
- Internal processes and communication are inconsistent.
- Customer retention is not where it should be.
- Employees aren't sure about the company's vision or brand promise.
- Customers aren't sure of the company's brand promise.
- There is occasional dissension or lack of trust within staff ranks.
- Employees and customers are unable to access upper management.
- There is failure to share best practices.
- There is little or no celebration of success.
- Employees may be in the wrong job.
- Employees feel a lack of appreciation.
- Training is inconsistent.
- There is little or no training for soft skills.
- Performance reviews are inconsistent.
- Employees don't feel as though they are part of a team.
- Employees have little or no authority to act independently to help the customer.

- There is a lack of motivation and an attitude of indifference.
- The company is operations-focused instead of customer-focused.

Do any of these symptoms seem familiar? This is by no means a complete list. You may be able to add more such symptoms of your own. Some of this is bad, and some of it is okay, but none of it contributes to delivering a *consistently positive customer experience.* If your customers and/or employees experience any of these symptoms, your company is operating within the cult of uncertainty. The only way to begin the transition out of uncertainty is to take a good, long look at where you are now. Admit and accept your current standing, and your journey begins with a plan to move out of uncertainty and into a cult of alignment—and ultimately to a *cult of amazement!*

The Keepers

- Most companies operate both internally and externally within the cult of uncertainty.
- There isn't consistent upward movement toward another cult. In fact, this cult is usually marked by *inconsistency.*
- It is easiest for employees to settle into a sense of complacency within this cult.
- It is easy to miss clues that there are problems with customers or employees.
- Your customers do not receive consistently above-average experiences. They don't know what to expect next. The outcomes may be good, intermittently, but they are never *consistently* good.
- Your customers may have no loyalty, even though they are technically satisfied with what you are giving them.

- Your employees may not have the tools or training they need to consistently deliver above-average experiences for customers—and they may never get them.
- The only way to begin the transition out of uncertainty is to take a good, long look at where you are now.

Chapter Five

ALIGNMENT

Once you've broken out of the cult of uncertainty, you can begin your journey toward *amazement*. Next in the process is the cult of alignment, which is marked by *movement in the right direction*.

Imagine for a moment that you are driving in the fast lane on a major highway. If your car's front end is out of alignment, the entire car may shake, and the ride can quickly become a dangerous one. Once the car gets its wheels aligned properly, going in a straight line is easy and smooth.

It's not so different in business. If the people on the front line don't understand the underlying value promise that is made to the customer, the entire company can suffer. Once you do the work necessary to get everyone aligned with the right message that connects to what that value promises—the right *mantra*—you can make headway and start moving forward.

IMPORTANT: A big part of alignment comes from training (both technical skills and soft skills), hiring right, and a consistent process. Examples of these are in later chapters. However, the *mantra* is the solidifying factor. Every employee must know it and understand it. It must be in place for alignment to work.

The transition from uncertainty into alignment is perhaps the most crucial phase any company has to go through to create high levels of service. I think of the journey as looking a little like what's shown in Figure 5.1.

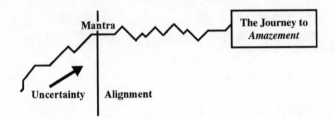

Figure 5.1 The Journey Out of Uncertainty

Look closely at the transition out of uncertainty and into alignment. Think about the work it takes to get out of uncertainty at the beginning of that roller-coaster ride discussed in Chapter 4. It takes a tremendous amount of effort to get up that first hill, and once you make it to the top, you're ready to go. Get over that hill, and you've got the momentum you need to handle the ups and downs of the journey that follows.

A big part of the hard work you must do to get to the top of that first hill—away from uncertainty and into alignment—is developing the mantra. As you ascend to the top of that first hill, you begin to develop a mantra that makes it easier to understand the direction in which you want to go. Finding that mantra takes effort, but it is the only way to begin the journey to *amazement*.

A mantra is a key phrase that is short and simple, yet manages to explain exactly what your values and goals are—so much so that when employees and customers hear it, they know exactly what the company is all about. A mantra keeps us focused, and the best mantras are the same for both employees and customers. However, it doesn't always have to be that way. The mantras can be different—as long as they complement each other.

Here Are Some of My Favorite Examples of Great Mantras

- The Ritz-Carlton preaches to their employees—and their guests—that the people who are lucky enough to work there are "ladies and gentlemen serving ladies and gentlemen." That defines the environment, the experience, and the *culture* they are constantly moving toward.

- Employees at Outback Steakhouses don't just serve steak: They serve "great food with NO RULES!" Again, that defines the environment, the experience, and the *culture* they are constantly moving toward.

- Employees who work at Volkswagen know that they are working "Aus Liebe Zum Automobil!" Translate that into English, and you'll know that the people who work at Volkswagen at all levels of the organization do what they do "Out of Love for the Automobile!" Once again, that mantra defines the environment, the experience, and the *culture* they are constantly moving toward. It also defines the customer's experience.

- At Avis Rent a Car, "We Try Harder" is their mantra and advertising slogan. They took the fact that they are not number one and exploited it, turning it into a brand promise. Both employees and customers get it. They may not be number one, but they want your business—and they will try harder to prove it to you.

One of my favorite mantras comes from the Beatles, who from the very beginning had a clear vision of what they wanted to achieve. Three short words helped to define their career as a band: Bigger than Elvis! The band adopted it at a point in their careers when they definitely were not yet bigger than Elvis Presley, or even worthy of being mentioned in the same sentence with him. But the phrase served as *north* on the Beatles' compass—the direction in which they knew they were going. Bigger than Elvis! Those three words had power, energy, and guidance, and their mantra saw the band through a lot of ups and downs.

Although this simple phrase may not seem to have much to do with customer service, it actually has a great deal to do with alignment. "Bigger than Elvis" is, in fact, what the scruffy-looking batch of overachievers delivered—and somehow continued to deliver—to fans in Liverpool and beyond. Four times the fun, four times the magic, four times the energy. Bigger than Elvis! Isn't that what they gave us?

The lesson is not just in the clarity and simplicity of the phrase "bigger than Elvis." It's also in the galvanizing effect the simple phrase had on the band itself. The band couldn't deliver the experience until they knew what it was supposed to be! They had to believe that they were *bigger than Elvis* internally before they could start giving that experience to their fans!

The Beatles had to map out and plan for a journey. Many times throughout their career, they were faced with questions and problems that were answered and solved by asking themselves: "Is this going to make us *bigger than Elvis?*"

What a Mantra Does

The right mantra marks the beginning of the journey to *amazement.* It may take a while to find, but once you locate it, you don't want to go back. You've found north on the compass, and that's the direction you want to go. You are in alignment—and like *amazement,* you can operate within this cult in a number of ways.

A person can be in alignment, have a personal mantra that connects to a sense of mission that affects that one person, and be a *force of one.*

A person or work team within an organization can have a mantra that hasn't yet been adopted by others. Such a work team becomes a *force within.* They can serve as outposts of *amazement* for the rest of the organization, or they can be ignored entirely, which is a shame. It's hard to say which is more likely to happen, because companies can be so very different.

An organization can have a mantra that defines the direction of the enterprise as a whole. Such an organization becomes a *force of many.*

Case Study: Progressive Car Insurance

When it comes to creating a powerful, fully *aligned* online experience for U.S. purchasers of automobile insurance, it's hard to beat Progressive Car Insurance. Their memorable brand promise "You could save hundreds!" is both impossible to miss and amply supported by the company's award-winning web site. Although this claim may simply sound like an advertising slogan, it truly is much more. It shows that that the company has the customers' interests at heart. To back it up, Progressive put together a web site that is totally customer-focused. They even show competitors' rates that can save the customer money. It's all about the customer!

To put the matter bluntly, Progressive's easy-to-navigate, easy-to-quote online experience is one of the most accessible and impressive outposts in all of cyber-commerce. That may sound like hyperbole until you take a close look at some of the accolades the company has received. Keynote Competitive Research, a leading industry analysis group, cited the web site's "improved functionality, security, and quality" and awarded Progressive the number one spot on its first-quarter 2008 Insurance Carrier Scorecard. Progressive has taken the top spot in 12 of the last 13 rankings from Keynote. Another outside evaluator, the Customer Respect Group, ranked Progressive's online experience as the best in its industry in March 2008 and noted that the company was "strikingly interactive and innovative, featuring RSS feeds, blogs and other features more commonly found on high-technology or retail websites."

Take a minute to visit Progressive's web site (www.progressive .com) and see for yourself whether the company's online experience lives up to its familiar mantra, "You Could Save Hundreds!"

Case Study: Enterprise Rent-A-Car

By all appearances, Enterprise Rent-A-Car shines when it comes to internal *alignment*. Its now-famous promise to consumers, "We'll pick you up," came into existence not as an edict from headquarters but as inspired improvisation from a frontline rental manager in Florida. The manager realized that a customer who needed a lift and got one would be more likely to rent again from Enterprise. The practice was later adopted company-wide and has emerged as a major competitive and strategic advantage for the company. Enterprise picks up some of its best management talent from inside its own organization; close to 100 percent of the company's management team began in Enterprise's management training program. Although some company mantras cross over and are identical from employee to customer, Enterprise is an example of an internal employee mantra that stands alone. The company's internal mantra for employees is "My Personal Enterprise."

Mike Hardhead Finds His Mantra

Mike Hardhead, CEO of WidgetBlue, took the sage advice of his former mentor, Harlan Love, and did a top-to-bottom analysis of his company—and himself. It was not quick or easy, but it was important, and he ended up being very glad that he did it.

Mike realized that the weakest link at WidgetBlue included Mike Hardhead himself. He realized that although he was the founder and CEO of a pretty good widget company, he was also the person responsible for instilling the wrong mantra at his company. As it stood, the unofficial mantra was "Don't get caught screwing up." No one really said it out loud, at least not to Mike's face, but it was in fact the driving motivation behind what just about everyone did at WidgetBlue.

When Mike started WidgetBlue, he had the drive and passion for the quality that was needed to get the company off the ground, and it helped him track down managers who were able to create some good internal processes at the company. Over time, the company grew, and growth created some hidden problems. Business was moving at a faster pace, almost too fast. Some employees couldn't handle the stress and were experiencing burnout. Mike and his managers were also stressed, and they were not always tolerant of employees who couldn't keep up with the pace. All of this led to WidgetBlue's delivery of a level of service that was *not consistently good.*

However, one employee on staff seemed to take a real joy in figuring out how to help WidgetBlue customers. That employee was Millie, and she had been on staff almost since the company was founded. When Mike asked her to explain why she thought her ratings on customer experience surveys were so high, Millie had an instant and persuasive answer.

"Well," she said, "I solve problems. That's what I do best. That's what they call me for, help with solving their problems, and that's what I really want to do for them. I keep going after the problem until it's solved. Don't you remember? That's what you told me we did at WidgetBlue on the first day I came to work here."

Millie ended up being an *outpost of amazement* for Mike and for WidgetBlue. He kept turning one phrase from his interview with her over and over in his head. Millie had said, "I solve problems," and she had smiled when she said it. She loved solving problems!

Wasn't that the foundation on which he started his company?

Wasn't that his original mission for his company?

Wasn't that the mind-set he wanted everyone in the company to go back to—finding the very best solutions for his customers' widget problems?

After three weeks of interviews with dozens of employees, including multiple discussions with Millie—his *force within*—Mike concluded that he himself was the source of his biggest problem at WidgetBlue. Mike Hardhead found his company's mantra, his company's version of *bigger than Elvis*!

Mike's mantra was three words long as well, and it, too, told people exactly what his company's focus was going to be. And like the Beatles' mantra, this mantra would have to become a reality internally before it could become something customers could experience. WidgetBlue's new mantra was simply WE SOLVE PROBLEMS.

What about You?

Try it now for yourself. Come up with your organization's internal and/or external mantra. It should be one sentence long. It can focus *solely* on the customer experience, such as Progressive's "You could save hundreds!" or *solely* on the employee experience, like "My personal Enterprise," or it can concentrate on both, such as the Ritz-Carlton's "Ladies and gentlemen serving ladies and gentlemen."

REMEMBER: The internal and external mantras do not have to be identical, but they *must complement one another.*

Making a mantra simple is not a simple process. It will take effort, both brainstorming and tweaking. You'll come up with a phrase, live with it for a while, and end up changing it. It can be a tough process, but once you get through it, you will have a clear message about your company that both your customers and your employees understand. *That* is alignment! Start moving toward the top of the hill right now by creating your first draft of a mantra. Be prepared to revise it over the next weeks and months.

Are You in Alignment?

The mantra lets your employees know and understand your company's vision and mission. Add the right training, structure, processes, and hiring practices, and you will find yourself operating in the cult of alignment.

If you're wondering when—or whether—you've made it to this next phase, then consider the following factors, clues that an organization has moved into the alignment phase:

- The organization has created a simple and clear vision—a brand promise or a mantra.
- All employees understand and are able to repeat the mantra.
- The company is hiring right, promoting right, and training right.
- Employee training is not an afterthought, and it does not focus solely on product or service details. Training in soft skills is included, and a separate and comprehensive training regimen focuses on fulfilling the brand promise to customers.
- The organization continuously assesses itself by surveying employees and customers.
- Everyone wants to improve. Business as usual is not good enough.
- Members of the company commit to improving the experience for employees as well as customers.
- The organization is moving toward being customer-focused rather than operations-focused.
- Both employees and customers know where they're supposed to be going.
- Both employees and customers *like* where they're supposed to be going.

By the Numbers

According to a recent study, six internal drivers affect an organization's ability to motivate employees to deliver a consistent brand experience. Money, surprisingly, is *not* the most important driver: "With employees, the important investments go beyond monetary compensation. Pay may be enough to get people in the door, but it's not enough to keep them, let alone to create true brand ambassadors." More important factors are people, processes, structure, access to information, and a participatory decision-making process.[1]

The Keepers

- The cult of alignment is marked by *movement in the right direction.*
- If your organization is operating within the cult of alignment, you have a mantra that instantly points people in the direction they want to go.
- Your mantra keeps people focused. It's a key phrase that is extremely short yet so simple that when employees and customers hear it, they know exactly what the company is all about.
- It's not uncommon for a company in alignment to have two different mantras—one for customers and one for employees. However, these mantras must complement one another.

Chapter Six

EXPERIENCE

The cult of experience is marked by *actions supporting the mantra that took hold in the cult of alignment.* To introduce this next step toward the *cult of amazement,* I'll tell you about a significant and memorable experience of my own.

Not long ago, my mom, my son, and I went skydiving for the very first time. What a blast! If you look in the dictionary under the word *exhilarating,* you may well find a picture of someone skydiving for the very first time. The sensation, at least for me, wasn't at all like falling. Actually, it was a lot like floating. My instructor told me we would be falling at a rate of about 130 miles per hour, so a feeling of falling was what I expected. The floating sensation came as a pleasant surprise.

Perhaps you're wondering why I'm sharing my skydiving story with you in a book about customer service. It's really a perfect example of our third cult, *the cult of experience*—because of the different ways that my mom, my son, and I each processed the initial experience of skydiving.

When we shared our memories and discussed the experience afterwards, we were surprised to find that each of us remembered something different about what had just happened. I remembered how the wind first hit me the moment I exited the plane. My mom had no recollection of that feeling. I remembered going through the clouds. My son didn't remember that at all.

When I talked to my instructor about this after my jump, he told me that it was not uncommon for different people to have very different memories and experiences about their first jump. He told me that it takes at least three or four jumps for your brain to take in everything of substance about the jump. "Do this several more times," he told me, "and you'll all have basically the same point of reference. As it is now, it's all so new that your brain can't yet comprehend everything about this experience."

It occurred to me that he was talking precisely about the difference between the third and fourth phases of our journey toward *amazement:* the difference between experience and ownership.

Right now, if you were to ask me, my mom, and my son to tell you what happens during a jump, you'd get three very different answers. We're still in the experience phase of skydiving; we're not yet in ownership. We aren't sure what we are going to experience the next time, although we hope it will be just as good as, if not better than, the first jump.

By the same token, if you were to talk to a WidgetBlue customer about the first time he interacted with Millie, that customer might not recall every positive element of the exchange accurately. All the customer knows is that it was a good experience. After the third or fourth interaction with Millie, he will get to know Millie and have a predictable, positive experience. He knows what he's going to get, and he looks forward to the quality of that exchange. In other words, the customer starts to *own* the experience. But experience itself must precede any kind of ownership.

Positive Experiences Gain Momentum

As you head toward the *cult of amazement,* positive experiences begin to become something more than one-time events; they begin to repeat themselves. They seem to start intermittently and then become more consistent and predictable. At some point, the customers and employees don't simply *hope* for these good experiences to happen; they *expect* them to happen. They have confidence in the company, and they know that their concerns will be addressed. This is the where the foundation experience becomes familiar enough to support the transition into ownership.

Although the experiences are usually good—or even great—this may not always be the case. It's not that complaints and problems never occur at the level of experience; they are just more likely to be resolved to the customer's satisfaction than they were in the realm of uncertainty. This is because the training is better, the tools are better, and the employee understands the brand promise—or mantra—that supports the focus on the customer. In addition, the customer has a basis of hope for a future positive outcome.

By the Numbers

"Customers who complain and are subsequently satisfied are up to 8% more loyal than if they had never had a problem."[1]

Mike Hardhead Changes Course

Just three months after his fateful encounter with Harlan Love, Mike Hardhead was giving his company plenty of evidence that they were now being led by a new kind of CEO. After years of harsh, sometimes unforgiving exchanges with employees who had made mistakes, Mike now seemed more interested in sharing stories than in assigning blame. Everywhere Mike went, he had stories to tell about best practices, innovation, and creativity. Some of the stories were old and went all the way back to his decision to establish WidgetBlue. Some of the stories were new and included examples of people doing things better internally or delivering on the promise of We Solve Problems for WidgetBlue's customers.

There was a feeling of change in the air at WidgetBlue. Mike was treating the managers better, and—not coincidentally— managers were treating their employees better. In part, this was because of a late-night call Mike had had with his old mentor Harlan Love, who reminded Mike that "treating employees like they're the customer" was an art—an art that Mike and his entire company could master.

Treat the employee like the customer—or even better!

"You must model the behavior that you want your employees to emulate," Mr. Love had told him. "You can't beat them up and then expect them to be nice to their customers. Once you give them a positive experience, they'll better understand how to act toward customers. Furthermore, if you want your customers to feel that your company is easy to do business with, then your employees had better feel that you and your managers are easy to work with first."

As a result of that conversation with Harlan Love, Mike started having different kinds of meetings with his managers. Instead of looking for the biggest mistake that had happened in each department since the last meeting, he was now asking questions like these:

- "How easy are we for *employees* to connect with?"
- "How easy are we for *customers* to connect with?"
- "What was the best thing that happened in your department this week?"
- "Who else should know about that?"
- "What can we do to repeat that kind of success?"

- "Who had the best idea in your department this week?"
- "Who else should know about that idea?"

In just three short months, WidgetBlue had begun to move away from a culture of blame and toward a culture of celebration. Every day, more and more WidgetBlue workers were doing what Mike was doing: looking for evidence of ideas that actually worked, both internally and externally, and looking for new places to put those ideas into practice. Suddenly, people at WidgetBlue were looking forward to team meetings and beginning to see them as a chance to share cool new ideas, concepts, and strategies. Some of the ideas were great, and some needed a little more work. But all of them were—for the WidgetBlue team—evidence of a new way of interacting with each other and with their customers. The goal now was clear: to solve problems—and to deliver a positive experience to the customer.

Initial Experiences: Starbucks

I wasn't sure what to expect the first time I ever set foot inside a Starbucks. I had heard about people paying a very high price for a cup of coffee at this place. I don't even drink coffee, but that's beside the point, because I wasn't even there for the coffee. I was there to meet a client, who had suggested this was a good place to have an early morning meeting.

After just a few minutes, I realized that there was something about the ambience of the place that made me feel perfectly comfortable holding a business meeting there. Maybe it was the music, maybe it was the staff, maybe it was the décor, or maybe it was the three or four customers working on their laptop computers. Who knows? But I began to feel as though I'd landed in the right place.

To pass the time until my client arrived, I ordered something other than coffee: hot caramel apple cider. I discovered that it was well worth the price I'd paid for it. It was delicious! While I was waiting, I also bought a newspaper and settled down to read it. By the time my client arrived, I was glad he had suggested Starbucks as a meeting place and more than willing to consider meeting there again.

There was total alignment—and the ability to follow through on it—at Starbucks. It came from the staff, from the product, and from the ambience. The company had a certain experience that they wanted to deliver to me. I had just encountered that experience for the very first time, and I liked it.

As a customer, I had just entered the cult of experience with Starbucks. I wanted to see if I'd have a good experience the next time, too. And after several more visits, my experiences had become predictable. I had confidence that they would always be good. I was feeling like a regular. I liked going to *my* Starbucks.

Initial Experiences: PayPal

The first time I heard about PayPal—a web site that offers a secure method for online purchases and cash transfers—I wasn't just dubious; I was scared. I worried that someone might steal my private financial information, and that the money I was trying to send to a vendor might never reach its intended target. I spent quite a long time setting up my account—more time, truth be told, than I really had meant to spend, or should have spent. I guess I was taking all that time because I wanted to be really, really, *really* sure that what I was doing was safe.

After about half an hour of watchful, vigilant double-checking, I hit the final key to finalize my PayPal account and then finalized my first purchase using the site.

It worked. And it was a whole lot easier than I had thought.

My merchandise arrived without incident the next day. And no unauthorized trails of cash were leaking out of my bank account. I began to think to myself, "You know, that really was pretty easy to use. Maybe there is something to this whole PayPal thing."

I had just entered the customer cult of experience with PayPal. I wanted to see if I'd have a good experience the next time, too. After a few more visits, I was a pro, taking only a minute or so to complete a transaction. I was moving from an initial experience of concern—or even fear—toward the positive experience of ownership.

The Online Experience

Operations like PayPal have raised the bar on the online experience and, indeed, on customer service as a whole. There's virtually no contact up front with any demonstrably human customer service personnel, and yet people flock to PayPal. How can that be? It happens for a very simple reason: When the people at PayPal designed their web site, they were completely focused on customers and on the experience the customers would take away from their encounter. Sites like PayPal, Google, Progressive Insurance, and many others are excellent examples of web sites that are customer-focused. We must learn to ask ourselves: Who are our people designing the organization's web site *experience* around—the end user or our own internal users? Internal tools should be designed with employee *experiences* in mind, of course, but something that the customer interacts with must be designed with the *customer's* experience in mind!

If your online touch points are not yet designed with the *customer's experience* in mind, you're not yet part of the cult of experience, because you're not customer-focused—you're operations-focused! And many others are *amazingly* customer-focused. In a world of technology, it is too easy to be complicated and cumbersome. The best Internet sites make it easy for the customer. The cult of experience is, after all, about the *customer's* experience.

Stuck in the Cult of Experience

Some companies manage to get their customers to the cult of experience—and then leave them there, because they're unable to deliver on their promises over time or meet future expectations. The cell phone industry comes to mind in this instance. All too often, consumers get their cool new phones, fall in love with the features, and start using the new technology in new ways. On the retail or sales level, we've had a positive experience. Then we have a service issue—and we find ourselves talking to someone at a call center.

Unfortunately, it is the call centers that have been giving the cellular phone industry a bad reputation. As customers, we may not take the initiative to change cell phone providers when we find ourselves stuck at the cult of experience—or, more likely, sinking back into the cult of uncertainty. In either case, we are certainly vulnerable to the prospect of a better and more consistent experience from a competing vendor.

When organizations are in alignment, the employees and customers are getting a promise of something to come—something that's almost *magical.* As the cult of experience develops, the organization begins to delivers on that promise and begins a natural, almost seamless progression into the cult of ownership (which you'll learn more about in the next chapter). The internal organization begins to pick up momentum, and customers begin the process of expecting—and receiving—more consistent outcomes. That all begins with the *experiences* people encounter as employees or customers.

The cult of experience is where we are when we say to ourselves, "I've seen some of the good stuff now, and I want my confidence in this organization to increase." That happens to both customers *and* employees. In fact, it *must* happen to employees first. It's the organization's job to allow people to continue the journey into ownership by giving them evidence that the good stuff they just saw wasn't a fluke.

Finding yourself in the cult of experience means that you:

- Have a personal sense of mission that relates to your job.
- Create an experience that relates to that mission.
- Know what your organization's mantra is (or your own personal brand promise for your customers), and you're getting reinforced at some level for fulfilling that mantra.
- Are starting to feel empowered.
- Receive positive feedback for trying to do the right thing.
- Have been recognized by a customer or fellow employee for your good work.
- Find ways to make the *process* easy for the customer, not just easy for the internal people, if you are involved in creating your organization's virtual or online experience. You are *customer-focused.*
- Find your customer has begun the process of expecting more from you—or, at a minimum, expecting more of the same.

In the journey toward the *cult of amazement,* typical day-to-day customer and employee experiences are positive. When these positive experiences become the norm, confidence starts to build. Once these experiences are predictable and expected, you are moving out of the cult of experience and into the cult of ownership.

The Keepers

- The cult of experience is marked by direct encounters with actions supporting the mantra that took hold in the cult of alignment.
- Treat the employee like the customer—or even better.

- Model the behavior you want the employee to show the customer.
- Start asking questions that focus on the experience. These questions tell the story, which is a wonderful way to teach others in the organization. Some of the questions might include:

  "How easy are we for employees to connect with?"

  "How easy are we for customers to connect with?"

  "What was the best thing that happened in your department this week?"

  "Who else should know about that?"

  "What can we do to repeat that kind of success?"

  "Who had the best idea in your department this week?"

  "Who else should know about that idea?"

- When organizations are in alignment, employees and customers are getting a promise of something to come. As the cult of experience develops, the organization begins to deliver on that promise and begins a natural, almost seamless progression into the cult of ownership.

Chapter Seven

OWNERSHIP

The cult of ownership—the next step in your journey to *amazement*—is marked by *a sense of belonging that arises from a series of predictable positive experiences in the cult of experience.* Ownership is the result of the process that great philosopher Aristotle was describing when he observed: *"We are what we repeatedly do. Excellence then is not an act but a habit."*

Can you remember when you set foot, for the very first time, in an apartment or house that you were *about* to move into? It was probably completely empty. There were no memories. It wasn't a *home* yet, even though the address might have technically been your legal place of residence. On your very first journey into that abode—wherever it was—you may have had a sense of possibility, but you definitely *didn't* have the sense of being at home.

Now, fast-forward six months. You've been living at this address over that time period. However, it's now more than just an address or a physical structure; it's home. You know where your dresser is; you've gotten dressed hundreds of times. You know where your bed is; you've gone to sleep in it every night for six months. Everything is familiar. A certain comforting sense of *predictability* has settled in, and it didn't happen by accident. It was the result of a series of *experiences* that support the idea that this place is home.

You're in the Right Place—and You Know You Want to Stay There!

I call that comforting sense of being in the right place—of belonging, of knowing what to expect next and liking it ahead of time—the *cult of ownership.* As an employee of an organization, ownership is the feeling you get from truly *belonging* in a place where you absolutely love to work—a place you look forward to going to every morning. Yes, some people really do feel that way about their jobs! That positive feeling is all about being able to *anticipate* the positive experiences you'll have working with others in the company, interacting with the company's customers, and completing certain aspects of the job that you truly enjoy. You have a sense—not just that you work at and for the company—but that you belong there. This is ownership.

Predictability and belonging are what ownership is about. At its highest level, ownership provides the momentum that takes both employees and customers to the highest cult, the *cult of amazement.* Entry into the cult of ownership is the natural extension of the organization's continuous engagement in the cult of experience.

The Power of the Process: Mike Brings Some Magic to WidgetBlue

I'd like you to think about the questions that Mike started to ask his management team at WidgetBlue while they were all still in the *experience* phase. As time went on, he refined them. Here's what they looked like after a few weeks:

- "How easy are we for employees to connect with?"
- "What did we do this week that *accelerated* the process of making it easy for employees to connect with management?"

- "How easy are we for customers to connect with?"
- "What did we do this week that *accelerated* the process of making it easy for customers to connect with and have their problems resolved by WidgetBlue?"
- "Who should know about that?"
- "What can we do to repeat that kind of success?"
- "What was your best idea this week?"
- "Who else should know about that idea?"
- "What did you do to reward that person?"
- "How can we *accelerate* adoption of that idea elsewhere?"

If management starts asking questions like these—not just once in a while, but on a regular basis—the questions and the answers they generate become pathways to positive outcomes. When employees know that these questions are going to be asked, they actually start to think about the answers ahead of time. More important, they try to create new and better answers to these questions *throughout their workday.* Essentially, they are proactively creating positive experiences for their internal and external customers.

At this stage, good experiences are happening, and they aren't happening by accident. They are happening *on purpose.* This is ownership at the highest level. In the ideal situation, management *accelerates* the ownership process by asking the right questions on a regular basis. That's why I call these kinds of questions *accelerator questions.*

Within just a few weeks, those kinds of questions had become part of the *routine* at WidgetBlue—part of Mike's constant search for *new* processes and *new* best practices that would help his company deliver on its promise: *We solve problems!* Mike quickly got into the *habit* of asking these types of questions at *every* meeting he held with his management team. And his managers did the same. Asking the *accelerator questions* on a regular basis reminded Mike and his employees that his brand promise, *We Solve Problems,* was not just a commitment to WidgetBlue's customers but a commitment to every single member of the WidgetBlue organization.

Moments of Magic, Moments of Innovation at WidgetBlue

In the spirit of those accelerator questions, Mike started giving his managers a special assignment. They were to call a meeting with everyone in their department. At that meeting, managers were to ask all employees in their department to share at least one story with the group about how they created what he called a Moment of Magic for one of their fellow employees or for a customer. He asked his managers to praise each and every employee who shared one of these stories. Furthermore, he wanted the managers to bring him the very best of what they heard—the cream of the crop.

As it happened, though, Mike wanted more than stories. He also wanted to hear great *ideas* from everyone at WidgetBlue. At these same meetings, the managers asked every employee to come up with an idea or suggestion that would improve their jobs, the company, or the customer's experience. These Moments of Innovation™ could be as simple as someone asking for a larger wastebasket or as detailed and complex as a suggestion that might save the company tens of thousands of dollars. It didn't matter if the ideas were good or bad; what mattered is that everybody was thinking about how to improve WidgetBlue.

A Moment of Magic is any positive contact with the organization that a customer or employee *experiences*. At its best, a Moment of Magic is *amazing*; at its worst, it's still above average.

Moments of Innovation are ideas for improving the organization at any level—for instance, cost savings, profit enhancement, overall efficiency, team or individual morale—or any other area that affects internal or external customers.

Mike knew that the stories he was asking for would have a powerful effect on his organization, regardless of whether a person's story ended up being circulated or a person's idea ended up being implemented. Mike knew that the very act of sharing stories about Moments of Magic as a group and the stream of ideas that were coming from everyone's Moments of Innovation would point the team in the right direction. He knew this because he had been listening once again to his mentor, Harlan Love, who had told him the secret to building great processes and a great team:

Use the best ideas. Share the best stories. Just be sure to reinforce the *participation in the process* that gave you the ideas and the stories. Everyone is to be praised for participating, regardless of how useful or practical their ideas and stories might be.

By the Numbers

According to a recent study by business and strategy consulting firm Bain & Co., 90 percent of senior managers see innovation as a "key source of future competitive advantage," but 67 percent of those same managers reported being dissatisfied with their company's ability to generate innovative ideas.[1]

Zappos: Ownership, Inside and Out

Imagine working for a company that gives employees the authority to resolve customer problems and entrusts them with the long-term task of improving the company over time. That's the culture at Zappos, a breakthrough online retailer that exemplifies *ownership* and has made a culture of internal and external innovation a reality in an astonishingly short period of time.

Zappos employees literally write the book on their company's culture. The *Zappos Culture Book*, which is rewritten once a year, is almost entirely employees' descriptions of their own vision of the company's inclusive, customer-obsessed, innovation-driven way of doing business. A portion of the 2007 edition reads: "We want to know what the Zappos culture means to you specifically at this point in time, and we expect different answers from different people."

According to Zappos chairman and founder Nick Swinmum, "You need as many eyes, ears, and hands working toward the same goal for themselves, not for someone else."[2] A better definition of *ownership* has yet to come down the pike.

Zappos is an online retailer unlike any other. It's known primarily for selling shoes, and the company offers free rush shipping and returns. You may not have bought shoes from Zappos.com yet, but my guess is that you or someone you know *will* buy shoes— or something—from this site at some point in the not too distant future. Ask an accountant about Zappos, and you'll hear about how the company has grown at a surrealistically fast pace.

By the Numbers

Online shoe retailer Zappos.com, whose reputation for customer service excellence is rooted in its *Wow Philosophy* culture, had virtually no sales in 1999, the year of its founding. In the year 2000, its gross merchandise sales total was $1.6 million; in 2006, the number was $597 million![3]

Zappos has indeed posted some eye-popping numbers. What's the secret? What made such astonishing growth possible? The answer is pretty simple. It is the ability to make customers and employees say *wow!*

Ask a Zappos *customer* about the company, and you're likely to hear a story about astonishingly high levels of customer service, supreme ease and confidence of ordering, and a no-hassle experience that consistently brings *repeat* purchases of shoes and accessories. Ask a Zappos insider what has contributed to the company's explosive growth, and you'll hear about the vital importance of the *experiences* customers encounter and about the culture that makes those positive experiences consistent and predictable. Let me share some remarks on this score from the company's CEO, Tony Hsieh.

> We've aligned the entire organization around one mission: to provide the best service possible. Online shopping can be a scary experience, especially if you're shopping for shoes. At Zappos, we believe that if we consistently strive to provide the best online experience possible, then we will succeed in the long term. Rather than focus on maximizing short-term profits, we instead focus on how we can maximize the service we provide to our customers. We want every interaction with every customer to result in the customer saying:"WOW"—so that they will become customers for life. . . . In addition to trying to WOW our customers, we also try to WOW our employees and vendors and business partners that we work with. . . . We believe that it creates a virtuous cycle, and in our own way, we're making the world a better place.[4]

Zappos has invested heavily in processes that deliver *ownership* both inside and out, and the company has great faith in the people who execute and improve on those processes. Hsieh writes: "In order for us to succeed as a service company, we need to create, maintain, and grow a culture where employees want to play a part in providing great service. I've been asked a number of times what the company's biggest asset is, and my answer is always the same: the culture".[5]

Hsieh puts his money where his mouth is. His company offers to buy employees out of their jobs. New hires who don't seem fully committed to Zappos's distinctive WOW philosophy are offered a cash bonus to leave the company. Yes, you read that right. If you are hired, and—at the completion of your orientation—you don't seem to get it or don't think you fit in, the company will pay you to go away.[6]

Translation: Zappos *only* wants employees who belong. They only want employees who will assume full *ownership of the company's mission and culture.* Hsieh knows that if his whole team won't assume *ownership* of that mission, his customers aren't likely to consider themselves customers for life. *In other words, customers won't enter ownership until the company does!*

"At Zappos, customer service isn't just a department. It's the entire company. Internally, we have a saying: We are a service company that happens to sell shoes. And apparel. And handbags. And accessories. And eventually just about everything else."[7]

By the Numbers

Online retailers who have created a *process* for delivering predictably above-average customer experiences—and have used those experiences to enter the cult of ownership—include Zappos, PayPal, and Amazon.com. All have experienced stunning growth, and Amazon's growth curve has been particularly striking. The company reached $5 billion in sales in eight years, a benchmark that eluded Wal-Mart for the first 20 years of its existence! All three online brands have created and continue to stimulate a strong customer-centric experience rooted in *ownership* of the online experience.[8]

Clues That Your Organization Is in Ownership

All of the clues that you are in alignment and experience, *plus*:

- Strong levels of employee engagement as the norm (not the exception) in the organization.
- Higher-than-average retention numbers among frontline employees.
- Formal internal *processes* that empower employees to fix problems.
- Regular discussion of Moments of Magic types of stories, as well as praise and/or rewards for people who contribute to those discussions.
- Regular discussion of Moments of Innovation types of ideas, as well as praise and/or rewards for people who contribute to those discussions.
- Regular use of questions that resemble *accelerator questions* in team meetings.
- Proactive, habitual preparation for those questions among employees.
- Deep concern at all levels of the organization for the quality of the customer experience.
- The ability to bounce back and *recover* quickly in situations where there's a challenge with a customer by *fixing* the problem with a sense of *urgency* and with the right *attitude*.

The Keepers

- The cult of ownership is marked by a sense of *belonging* that arises from a series of predictable positive experiences in the cult of experience.
- Entry into the cult of ownership is the natural extension of continuous engagement in the cult of experience.
- Build *accelerator questions* into your meetings.

- A Moment of Magic is any positive contact with the organization that a customer or employee experiences. At its best, a Moment of Magic is *amazing*; at its worst, it's still above average.
- Moments of Innovation are ideas for improving the organization at any level, for instance, cost savings, profit enhancement, overall efficiency, team or individual morale, or in general, any area that affects internal or external customers.

Chapter Eight

AMAZEMENT

T he cult of *amazement* is marked by *a sense of loyalty and belonging* within a clearly defined community of insiders, as well as a strong desire to *recruit others* into that community—either as an employee or as a customer. In other words, customers and employees in this cult become *evangelists.*

Are You an Egghead?

Maybe you've heard the following saying: "There are two kinds of people in the world: those who divide the world into two kinds of people, and those who don't." When it comes to barbecuing, I suppose I'm one of the former, because I definitely divide the world up into two kinds of people: those who have, and love, a Big Green Egg and those who don't.

A Big Green Egg is a state-of-the-art outdoor cooker incorporating both ancient Japanese design and modern, high-tech ceramic technology. It's a great leap forward in barbecue technology. The product, the company, and its impressive support network combine to create a *predictable positive customer experience* among barbecue fans, time and time again.

Do Big Green Egg customers ever experience problems? Of course they do. But the quality of the experience they *usually* receive, in terms of both customer support and the use of the product, easily overshadows the occasional problem. As a result, the customer is eager to get back to the *typical good experience* as soon as possible.

> The Big Green Egg web site (www.BigGreenEgg.com), which I frequently visit, features clear, professional-quality videos that address the most common questions and challenges faced by customers. The company also does a great job of connecting users with helpful Internet forums and retail outlets that can help them address virtually any problem. *The engaged community of Big Green Egg users is a major resource for newcomers—and a major competitive advantage for the company!*

As it happens, I'm an evangelist for the Big Green Egg. How would you know that? Well, I could share my obvious passion for barbecuing on the Big Green Egg. You'd see how much I enjoy cooking for my friends and family. Then I might tell you about the product itself: its lifetime warranty, its ability to move from low heat to high heat quickly, its versatility, its capacity to do things that other outdoor cookers don't do, such as baking cornbread. If you were *really* lucky, you might come to my house and enjoy the privilege of eating something I'd cooked on my Big Green Egg, at which point you'd notice that the Egg delivers meals that simply taste better than meals prepared on any other outdoor cooker.

None of that, of course, would replace the *experience* of cooking on the Big Green Egg. That's the main thing I'd want you to do. Cook on it!

That's true *evangelism*: getting you to take action. Once you use or purchase a Big Green Egg, your journey toward *amazement* would begin. Here's what the beginning of that journey typically sounds like:

> "Every legend you may have heard about the Green Egg, an other-worldly looking green ceramic cooker that is supposed to deliver the most perfect barbecue ever, appears to be true. Testers spent weeks in trials, cooking everything from brisket to ribs, and the results astonished seasoned cooks and beginners alike. . . . All [of our testers] admitted it took a little bit to master the ratios of fuel to air needed to maintain temperatures over longer times, but said the results were well worth the effort. Several appreciated helpful tips on the www .biggreenegg.com online forum."[1]

Astonished!

Once you *experience* cooking something on the Egg, you'd realize that no book or article could possibly convey the reality of the situation. You'd be—in the words of the *Wichita Falls Times Record News*—*astonished.* You'd discover that the Egg delivers an unparalleled barbecuing experience, one that allows even rank amateurs like me to serve what measures up to professional-level, mouth-watering barbecue. You'd discover that the Egg makes it almost impossible to mess up a cookout. You'd start thinking about buying one for yourself. And once you'd bought one, you'd eventually start suggesting that other people buy a Big Green Egg.

That would make you a special kind of customer: an Egghead. I'm an Egghead, because I've convinced a number of my friends to buy a Big Green Egg. I want others to have the same great experience I have had. I want others to join the community. *Eggheads love to recruit other Eggheads!* It's the fantastic product and the excellent customer support that come together to create such an *amazing* overall experience. That's the power of the *cult of amazement*.

And here's why it works: The company walks its talk. The company's founder, Ed Fisher, has created a simple brand promise and mantra: *World's best smoker and grill.* It's just that simple.

Lots of companies claim they are the world's best this or that. Yet very few companies have an army of *evangelists* who are passionately engaged in persuading other people to take *action* and try the product themselves. What qualifies the Big Green Egg for the *cult of amazement* is *not* its (albeit true) claim, but rather its army of evangelists.

Big Green Egg is not like other companies. They are not just in the business of manufacturing barbecue equipment; they are also in the business of creating and supporting a *community* of passionate evangelists, both inside and outside the organization.

"Ed Fisher cites the satisfaction of current EGG® owners and their unbridled enthusiasm and desire to convince everyone they know to cook on an EGG accounts for a good share of the Company's success. These 'EGGheads' have been the Company's strongest marketing tool with their effective one-on-one selling to friends and neighbors. Many excellent suggestions for product improvements have come from Big Green Egg owners based on their cooking experiences with the EGG. The Company recognizes the value of these loyal customers and the contributions they make to the success of the Big Green Egg."[2]

The *Cult of Amazement* Allows for Forgiveness

Eggheads have so much enthusiasm for the product that they are almost always willing to work through any problems that they might have with the Big Green Egg—because they *trust* the company. The same is true for virtually any organization that has this kind of relationship with its customers. If a customer experience is extremely positive and predictable, then customers will be willing to give a company a second chance when there are problems.

Guaranteeing *both customers and employees* as members of the *cult of amazement* is almost an insurance plan for any problems that might arise. Whenever there's any kind of setback, and you're so good that people come to *expect* great things from you as a matter of course, you have earned the right to *stay in the game* to fix the problem. And *fixing* such problems creates even more confidence on the part of your evangelists!

> "Brand loyalty and employee loyalty are both real assets, even if [they are] not reflected on balance sheets and income statements. Just look at Apple Computer with respect to products and DaVita, the kidney dialysis company, which has few open nursing positions because it is a great place to work. As Herb Kelleher of Southwest Airlines recognized long ago, if you take care of your people, they will take care of the customers, who will keep coming back, which will make the shareholders happy. It is all interrelated."[3]

Mike Gets It Right

One year after his trade show encounter with Harlan Love, Mike found himself at the helm of an *amazing* organization. Thanks to his ability to change the way he communicated; his consistent focus on a single, compelling mantra, *We Solve Problems*; and his willingness to ask questions he didn't yet know the answers to (like the *accelerator* questions you saw in Chapter 7), Mike's managers, frontline employees, and customers were all happier.

He knew the managers were happier because they'd stopped dodging him in the hallways.

He knew the frontline employees were happier because the retention numbers were up dramatically.

And he knew the customers were happier because they were returning in droves, offering praise and constructive suggestions on the new interactive WidgetBlue web site and user forums, and giving WidgetBlue plenty of golden referrals.

In just one year, Mike had revived a dormant culture of innovation and service at WidgetBlue. The reemergence of that culture led some of Mike's previous customers to reconsider their decision to leave the company, to get back in the fold, and to eventually become *evangelists* for the company.

WidgetBlue's customers were willing to give the company another chance, because they liked the experiences they'd come to expect from Mike's team. Although customers still have the occasional problem with WidgetBlue, they now had every reason to expect that WidgetBlue would keep its promise to *solve problems* and exceed their expectations. Plenty of un-solicited testimonials were showing up on various WidgetBlue-related web sites. There was now a real, live community of WidgetBlue fans—and it was growing every day.

As if all that weren't enough, WidgetBlue's margins were up. It turned out that customers who were willing to evangelize on his company's behalf were more willing to consider purchasing his upscale new products and to commit to long-term deals with the company. If you were to ask Mike why that is, he'd give you a short but profound answer: "We solve problems, both inside and outside the organization."

Price and the Evangelist

As Mike's story suggests, you don't have to have the lowest prices in your industry to gain entry into the *cult of amazement*. In fact, many organizations that operate in this arena are somewhat higher on the price scale than the rest of the market.

It's not that price doesn't matter. It does, and there is always a breaking point. However, being in the *cult of amazement* affords you the opportunity to sell on much more than price!

By the Numbers

Consumers who feel that they have a strong relationship with a company are, as a group, less likely to experience price sensitivity. This may help to explain how brands like Macintosh and Victoria's Secret can retain and even expand market dominance during tough economic times.[4]

A study in the banking industry determined that at a major New York bank, customers with frequent unresolved service problems were twice as likely to be dissatisfied with charges and fees levied by the bank than customers who had experienced only intermittent service problems. Why? Customers who had a better experience with the bank were more likely to see that the value in the relationship was more important than the fees that the bank charged.[5]

Disney Overcomes Internal Price Sensitivity

We've looked at price sensitivity among *consumers* who are operating at the *cult of amazement*. What about employees? Are they driven only by the money you pay them? People have to make a living; however, the paycheck may become a little less important if there are other positive parts to the job.

You probably already know that Disney World and Disneyland are legendary as magical tourist and vacation destinations. But did you know that Disney's employee compensation plan is considered by many to be somewhat low? It's true. How is it possible, then, for Disney to post the stellar employee retention record it has generated over the years at its theme parks and resorts? And how do they get the employees—or cast members, as they're known within the parks—to deliver such a consistently magical experience when they aren't paying top dollar for the top people? The answer is simple and, at the same time, profound: *People who work at the Disney theme parks know they work in a special place and want to keep working there.* They are part of a special kind of team.

Part of the reason for Disney's success in this area appears to be its ability to inspire a sense of *belonging* in its employees, a feeling that they are a part of not just *any* team, but a unique kind of team. The people who work at Disney are not just reporting to work every day. They are on a mission—one that supports and values both individual and team contributions and appeals to each employee's beliefs, values, and identity. In fact, if this *weren't* the case, the Disney organization wouldn't be able to offer high-priced consulting services on team building and employee retention to other organizations eager to get a little of the Disney magic to rub off on *their* workforces.

What the Disney organization has accomplished and systematized makes both people sense and bottom-line sense. It is also completely consistent with a survey by Challenger Outplacement Council, a study that identified three factors that were *more important* than financial rewards in motivating and retaining employees:

1. Recognition/appreciation
2. Independence
3. Contribution to the company

Salary actually came in *fourth* in importance. The moral of the compensation question is the same as the moral of the pricing question: Once employees undergo an *experience* that is positive and predictable, are appreciated for their efforts, and feel they are making a contribution to the company, money can become less of a factor. This is not to say that money isn't important; it is, of course, because people have to earn a living. But money becomes a part of the entire experience, not the most important or single motivating factor.

By the Numbers

- It's estimated that the Disney organization retains 85 percent of its theme park workers annually, a very high figure in that industry.[6]
- The Disney organization employs more than 50,000 people; approximately 1,600 work at or above the level of vice president. Of those executives, 14 percent have been with the organization for at least 20 years, a remarkably high number. In a recent survey by *BusinessWeek*, Disney was named one of the 10 best companies in America for launching a career.[7]

You've Never Been to Tony's? You Should Go!

One of my favorite personal examples of an organization that operates in the *cult of amazement* is Tony's, an upscale restaurant in St. Louis, Missouri. Tony's has earned a lasting reputation for excellence in dining. *The people who work at Tony's know they work someplace special, too.*

Sometimes it's tough to get a reservation unless you call well in advance, and there's a reason for that. Tony's delivers an absolutely top-notch dining experience and truly impeccable service. In fact, Tony's operates at the highest level of the *cult of amazement.* All they have to do is *meet the customer's expectations* to keep people coming back and recommending the restaurant to their friends. That's how good they are!

"I had heard that this was a nationally known restaurant. And now I know why. The service was INCREDIBLE. We never mentioned that it was my birthday, but they brought me dessert and wished me a happy birthday in their very subtle way (they overheard my husband and me talking). Tony comes around to all of the tables, which I found charming. It definitely is a conservative restaurant, but the food was incredible. I've never had such *amazing* food or service before. It's definitely expensive, but I thought it was well worth it. Not an everyday kind of place—special occasions! I highly recommend it."—*An online review of Tony's*

iPod Builds Communities of Evangelists

Apple's iPod is another example of evangelizing in the *cult of amazement.* How many people do you know who love their iPods, take their iPods everywhere, and evangelize on behalf of their iPods? There are currently 150 million iPods in circulation, and that number continues to grow. Millions of people identify themselves as members of the iPod, iPhone, or Apple community. And like the Big Green Egg fan base, many iPod, iPhone, and Macintosh users tend to divide the world into two camps: those who use Apple products and those who don't.

Apple works hard to build communities—and evangelists—with the iPod. The company successfully pursues strategically important consumer segments—such as the student market—to gain market share. According to an October 22, 2007, article on the AppleInsider.com web site, survey results from independent monitoring service SurveyU revealed that "Apple is gaining ground [in the higher educational market] thanks to the tandem of its discounted student purchase programs and its iPod halo-effect. The survey of 1000 online participants earlier this month found that the success of the Mac maker's back-to-school and educational programs are a significant contributor to its on-campus momentum, with more than 4 out of 5 (83 percent) of Mac-owning students having purchased their Mac under a student plan that included a free iPod." Apple finds ways to get students to use the product and keeps them using with the *experience.* They are experts at building communities.

Students aren't the only people on college campuses who are engaged and *amazed* by the iPod experience. Georgia College and State University is using the iPod as part of the curriculum. Course materials are loaded onto IMac computers where students dock their iPods to download information and assignments. For example, in a course titled "War, Politics and Shakespeare," audio recordings of music, historical speeches, and more were loaded on to the students' iPods as a learning tool. The university's iPod work has led to the formation of a special group of evangelists, known as iDreamers, who have developed even more uses for the iPod as an educational resource.[8]

That's *amazement*—and evangelism—at its best!

Harlan Love Sells Out

Two years after his encounter with Harlan Love at an industry trade show, Mike received a call from his former mentor. Harlan had been watching Mike's progress at WidgetBlue with interest and admiration, and he was eager to talk—in person—about what he called a strategic matter.

"I'm not a young man anymore," Mr. Love said at the beginning of the meeting. "In fact, I'm ready to retire. I've been looking for someone I could pass my business off to, Mike—and I'm wondering if you'd consider setting up a structure that would allow you to buy my company."

Mike smiled and agreed on one condition: that Mr. Love stay on as chairman emeritus and help Mike spread the word about the journey to *amazement* that makes great things possible.

Clues That Your Organization Is in *Amazement* Include All of the Clues That You Are in Alignment, Experience, and Ownership, *Plus* . . .

- Your customers act as evangelists for the organization.
- Your employees act as evangelists for the organization.
- The experience you deliver may not be perfect, but it is consistently and predictably good—even above average.
- Customers and employees expect you to meet your own standards, and they trust that those standards are high.
- You have high employee-retention numbers.
- Your organization exceeds people's expectations in its own unique way.
- Your real competition is yourself.

The Keepers

- The *cult of amazement* is marked by *a sense of loyalty and belonging* within a clearly defined community of insiders and the strong desire to *recruit others* into that community, either as an employee or as a customer.
- In this cult, customers and employees become *evangelists*. That means they are not only loyal but also committed to taking *action* that gets others to join the community.
- Evangelists *want* the company to get things right.
- Evangelists inside the company (employees) do what they have to do to make things right.
- Companies operating in the *cult of amazement* have created a second-chance insurance policy. If a customer or employee has a problem, they are far more likely to give the company a second chance to make things right. And these problems are solved in a way that reestablishes confidence—and even makes the relationship between the company and the customer even stronger.

- In the *cult of amazement,* the value that the company creates allows it to sell on much more than price. In fact, many organizations that operate in this cult have somewhat higher prices than their competitors.
- Companies operating within the *cult of amazement* have higher employee-retention rates.
- In the *cult of amazement,* employees may consider their paycheck to be a part of their employment experience—not the single motivating factor.

At its highest level, the *cult of amazement* makes employees and customers divide the world into two groups: people who are part of your community and everyone else.

Part Three

THE JOURNEY TO *AMAZEMENT*

Chapter Nine

WHAT THE JOURNEY LOOKS LIKE FROM THE INSIDE

THE INTERNAL MARCH TO *AMAZEMENT*

> "The more people are valued, the more connected they become. It perpetuates itself."
> —Bruce Nordstrom, chairman of the board, Nordstrom, Inc.[1]

As we have seen, the journey from uncertainty to *amazement* relies on direct experience and is propelled by special interactions I call Moments of Magic. I introduced the idea of a Moment of Magic in Chapter 2 and defined it as the experience of receiving above-average service. These moments give you the feeling that the organization that is serving you *values* you, and your direct experience steadily increases your confidence in them. Moments of Magic make it possible for you as a customer to buy into the goals and the vision of the company.

It should come as no surprise that these above-average customer experiences don't happen by accident. They take place as the result of great leadership.

> "The true leader serves. Serves people. Serves their best interests, and in doing so will not always be popular, may not always impress. But because true leaders are motivated more by loving concern than a desire for personal glory, they are willing to pay the price."
>
> —Eugene B. Habecker[2]

In fact, a Moment of Magic—an above-average experience— typically takes place as the result of someone's consistent and patient focus on the complex task of consistently delivering Moments of Magic to *internal* customers—so they can, in turn, consistently deliver Moments of Magic to *external* customers.

Believe it! This kind of experience must be *modeled* internally before it can be delivered on a consistent basis across the organization.

Occasionally, I come across human resource employees, corporate executives, and even entrepreneurs who omit or minimize this internal modeling part of the equation. Not overtly, of course. They say the right things and talk about how important their employees are to the company's mission. Yet sometimes they *act* as though the way that management treats employees doesn't affect the service their teams deliver to outside customers.

It's not that these people aren't interested in what happens inside their companies; they are perhaps simply too far removed from the people whose job it is to exceed customer expectations on a regular basis. I am here to tell you, however, that Harlan Love's advice to Mike in Chapter 4 is a *nonnegotiable prerequisite* of the journey to *amazement*: "Treat your employees the way you want your customers treated—maybe even better!"

Unfortunately, some executives don't realize the importance of this principle.

Why the Disconnect?

It's not hard to understand why this happens. Human nature has much to do with it. After all, it is human nature to want to point out problems when they occur, perhaps even in a dramatic way that is difficult to ignore. It's human nature to be a little aggressive when you see someone making mistakes. Even though this isn't the way that managers imagine themselves or their employees treating customers, it is still very common for them to take an aggressive approach with employees, for instance, by dressing them down with intensity for a mistake, either in private or (even worse) during a team meeting.

By the same token, it is human nature to avoid asking questions about how employees feel and to try to skip ahead to the desired *outcome:* a positive customer experience. It's human nature to expect people to simply carry out the tasks in their job description—which often include listening to customers and treating them well, showing pride in the organization, being enthusiastic, demonstrating a positive attitude, and taking full advantage of an opportunity to exceed a customer's expectations—without giving them reasons and incentive to do so. After all, isn't that what we are paying them for?

While such feelings are understandable, we should put ourselves in the employee's position for a moment. By doing so, we will notice that it is *also* human nature to resent the times when senior management may not listen to *us* or treat *us* well. At times like this, it becomes difficult for us to have or show pride in the organization. We may lose our enthusiasm for our job. When we harbor these kinds of resentments over time, we may have difficulty treating customers well, or we may even stop trying altogether.

What Are We Demonstrating?

Whether managers and executives like it or not, they are *demonstrating to team members exactly how they want customers to be treated* when they interact with those very team members. For many managers, that's a sobering thought, but it's an undisputable fact. (By the way, if you happen to know a manager who needs a reality check on this subject—leave this book on his or her desk!)

The truth of the matter is that we cannot badger, harass, intimidate, or humiliate employees into delivering Moments of Magic. We must listen to them, treat them with respect, and give them a sense that they have some kind of control over the world they encounter at work. Only then can we expect team members to listen to customers, treat customers with respect, and give them the excellent service and experience they deserve.

In the end, the organization will only deliver to customers the *Amazement* that we are willing to build into the experience of our employees. If we consistently exceed the expectations of employees, they will consistently exceed the expectations of our customers. If we don't, we shouldn't expect to enter the *cult of amazement.*

> "You have to perform at a consistently higher level than others. That's the mark of a true professional. Professionalism has nothing to do with getting paid for your services."
>
> —Joe Paterno[3]

Real Life *Internal Amazement:* Wainwright Industries

I work with many different types of clients, and once in a while I run into people who are skeptical at some level about how realistic it is to build a service philosophy—and a business—on the principle of *delivering* Moments of Magic to employees first. Some say it seems too expensive or too time-consuming. It may seem not to be a fit with their industry, their business, or their personality. Most of the people who feel this way— whether they say so or not—seem to believe that one can simply *expect* employees to deliver such moments to customers—and then step back and watch it happen. That's an unrealistic expectation.

One of my favorite examples of a company that shows exactly how realistic and strategically sound it is to adopt an employee-focused business philosophy is Wainwright Industries. Wainwright is a provider of "custom-fit, cost-effective, precision manufacturing solutions" and a major manufacturer of aerospace, information technology, and home security components. Any discussion of Wainwright Industries has to begin with its extraordinary CEO and chairman, Don Wainwright. While at the helm of the company, Don emerged as an internationally recognized leader in the areas of team building, quality, efficiency, and of course, customer service. He has won numerous awards for his innovative management, manufacturing, and team-based innovations, most notably the Malcolm Baldrige National Quality Award. In 2004, Don was chosen by President Bush to serve as chairman of the Manufacturing Council of the United States.

I could go on at length about the honors and awards that Don and his company have won over the years, but that's not why we're here. I want to highlight Don's work because he has somehow— seemingly against all odds—managed to maintain a thriving manufacturing business in the "heart of America" (to quote the Wainwright Industries web site). He's done this at a time when most such businesses have located manufacturing facilities overseas to capture the supposed competitive advantage of cheap labor. If you are wondering how he's done it, here's a big clue: Don Wainwright treats his people the way he wants them to treat the customer—maybe even better.

"Jack Welch uses only three indicators to run giant General Electric. . . . The most effective and only numbers he needs to know are, in order of importance: employee satisfaction, customer satisfaction and cash flow."

—Don Wainwright[4]

The Challenge

To get a sense of how Don put this principle of employee satisfaction into action, you have to rewind to the late 1970s and early 1980s, during a time when foreign competition in the components industry forced Don to face a market reality: His company was losing its competitive edge. Sales had dropped from $5 million to $3 million, and the company's facilities were operating only three days a week instead of five. Tensions between labor and management were high. So Don decided to make some fundamental changes at his company.

"The world is changing, and if it is changing faster than you are, then you have real problems. If you don't stay engaged and stay involved, issues will get out of control."

—Don Wainwright[5]

The theme of changing his company faster than the outside world could change became a passion for Don Wainwright. And make no mistake: These were big changes!

He started by erasing the supposed gap between labor and management by doing away with time cards, putting everyone on salary, and changing frontline job titles to "associate." In one of his bolder moves, Wainwright instituted a strict dress code. New uniforms were to be worn by everyone up and down the line, regardless of his or her status as labor or management. The standard attire now consisted of black slacks and a white pinstripe shirt bearing the team member's name on one side and the logo Team Wainwright on the other. The company instituted an attention-getting profit-sharing program, and Wainwright's books were opened for anyone in the company to see. Although some of the changes initially met with resistance, everyone eventually bought into the transformations that Wainwright was launching.

Don Wainwright also made a strong financial commitment to training his people in skills that they could market elsewhere if they ever had to leave the company. He made it clear to his people that while he was not in a position to make promises, his first choice was to develop and reassign rather than lay off employees. But if people did have to be let go, he wanted them to possess skills that would give them an advantage in the job market.

Why bother with any of these changes? Wainwright knew that the turnaround he had in mind would be impossible if employee satisfaction was low or even mediocre. He wanted it to be positively off the charts. He was a man on a mission, and he knew that *employee satisfaction must precede customer satisfaction.*

Before too long, the tension between labor and management had disappeared. Everyone was now in *alignment* and tied into Don's mantra, which was all about improving quality. "Quality," he likes to say, "is perseverance and character."

The Big Change

The change that Don made that was nearest and dearest to my heart was the implementation of his suggestion program. The concept was simple, yet its implications were felt throughout the company and, indeed, in every market where his company competed. In short, the concept was this: Every member of Team Wainwright had a weekly obligation to submit, in writing, one idea on how the company could improve. Any idea was acceptable. That went for everybody. No exceptions!

The policy was phenomenally successful. The results were nothing short of astonishing.

Do the numbers yourself. Wainwright Industry today has 250 employees. That means that, by the end of the year, the employees turn in approximately 12,500 suggestions! That's a huge number. Of course, not every one of those ideas is a good one. Perhaps the company puts only 50 or 100 of those ideas into practice. But here's the surprise: In the long run, the 12,400 ideas the company *doesn't* use are just as important as the 100 or so that it does *because the process of generating those 12,500 ideas gets everybody thinking, all the time, about the best ways to improve what Wainwright does!* That certainly supports Don's focus on quality, and we should also recognize how well it supports the people in the company. Not only does the policy pave the way for the minority of ideas that are actually used—some of which are excellent and on a par with the most expensive management consulting advice available—but it has a massive positive effect on corporate culture. At Wainwright, people get used to thinking that their opinion actually matters. What a concept!

Here's a brief summary of some of the *amazing* things Don's company has accomplished since implementing this one-idea-a-week policy.

- Employee satisfaction soared.
- First and foremost, Wainwright survived, and thrived, following a shakeout that left many of its competitors out of business.
- Employee attendance hovered around the 99 percent level.
- Customer satisfaction levels reached 95 percent.
- Company revenues soared past the $100 million mark.

Wow! That's an internal Wow, by the way, the kind of Wow that comes from someone who loves where he or she works and really doesn't want to work anywhere else. That's the kind of Wow that makes it possible for an employee to deliver more and better Wow experiences to the customer.

Here are some questions to consider. Could Don Wainwright have managed that turnaround without listening to and engaging his people? Could he have done it if he'd started complaining about how expensive it was to make the changes he had to make and if he'd found reasons to postpone those changes? Could he have done it without creating a bond of trust between the company and its employees? Chances are that he would not have been able to do so under those circumstances. Don Wainwright is one of the best contemporary examples of a leader who responded to a competitive challenge by getting the team in *alignment* and marching that team toward the *cult of amazement*.

> "Look out for people and their best interests. Treat people with dignity; show confidence in their ability. Listen carefully to what people are saying. Deliver on the promises you make. Be authentic and share yourself openly. Feel free to admit your own mistakes. Include others in decision making processes. Always tell the truth."
>
> —Don Wainwright, on how to build trust in an organization[6]

If you use Don's strategy of requiring all employees to share an idea each week (and there is no reason not to), make it a point of offering *public praise* at team meetings for the inevitable great ideas that you do end up using. There is no better way to transform a team—and no better way to get the team into alignment quickly—than to prove you are willing to listen to its members and give them input into what happens in their world! Who knows? They may just start listening to *customers* in the way that you have been listening to *them*.

Five Critical Pathways

Employees will sign on for—or ignore—your organization's journey out of uncertainty based on five critical factors.

- *Little things that mean a lot.* What daily messages are we sending to the team about their value to the organization? Notice how Don Wainwright emphasized the value he placed on his people by, for instance, upgrading them to be called associates. It may have just been a title change, but it was something that made a difference to the people who received it.

- *Problem solving and recovery.* Do we turn our own employees' Moments of Misery into Moments of Magic? When I train corporate teams, I make it a point to identify the top three Moments of Misery that they are likely to run into with their internal and external customers. Then we work on the best strategies for resolving those challenges. Notice, too, how Don Wainwright took action on his own employees' grievances first before addressing any customer issues—or demanding that they do so.

- *Opportunity knocks.* Are we ready and willing to improve on a fair, average, or acceptable experience—without the employee having to ask for it? Notice how Wainwright took the initiative to improve people's pay and profit-sharing plans.

- *Proactive culture.* Do we anticipate employee needs and problems—and address them as early as possible? Notice how much emphasis Wainwright put on *generating ideas for improvement* from his team members, improvements that could come about in any area of the organization they wished to focus on!

- *The Art of Wow.* Do we deliver experiences that make employees stop and think, "That's *amazing*! I can't believe I *get to* work here!" Wainwright's choice to open up the company's books certainly qualifies as a Wow moment, and there have been many others.

As you can probably tell, Don Wainwright is one of my favorite examples of a leader who really walks his talk when it comes to delivering on promises to employees. He instills the kind of quality focus and loyalty to the organization that make Moments of Magic a predictable reality in his team's interactions with customers. Fortunately, Wainwright Industries is not the only company that proves that a business strategy based on delivering *internal amazement* can be practical and realistic. Here are some of my other favorite examples.

Mid-America Motorworks

Mike Yager has parlayed an immense enthusiasm for Corvettes and a $500 personal loan into a one-of-a-kind business. His company, Mid-America Motorworks, delivers parts and accessories to the global and often upscale community of classic Corvette (and now Volkswagen) enthusiasts. Mike founded what eventually became Mid-America in 1974. He takes a pass on titles like president and founder and instead prefers to refer to himself as chief cheerleader. His company's mantra is "Pursue Your Passion Here"—and that's exactly what employees at Mid-America do. They're all passionate about cars, and they're all passionate about the customer experience they deliver. They take their cue on both scores from the chief cheerleader.

I am proud to have Mike as one of my clients. At one point, the Mid-America team was suiting up every Tuesday in black polo shirts that had the *Moments of Magic* logo. They met to talk about what went right that week in interactions with *external and internal* customers. Every Moment of Magic experience— whether the recipient was *inside or outside* the company—was recorded and circulated in the company newsletter. The very act of *sharing* these stories on a weekly basis emphasizes to everyone that a critical part of the job at Mid-America Motorworks is *creating* these stories!

> "The key to our success is built upon a simple principle: treat people fairly."
> —Mike Yager, Chief Cheerleader, Mid-America Motorworks

Does your company have a weekly meeting in place for the team to share Moments of Magic that have happened to both inside and outside customers? Are you passionate about sharing those stories? Do you circulate them company-wide and praise the people behind them, as Mike Yager does?

Open.com

This Boston-based software company, headed by CEO Morris Panner, has built into its culture the powerful routine of what they call the morning huddle. This is a chair-free, open-mike meeting in which the company as a whole (and not just top management) sparks a discussion that shares the high points and low points of the previous day. In other words, the team has a few minutes to share what's working and what's not.

As Panner explained, "The first thing people (usually) do in a meeting is tune out. They sit down in a chair, and they have that passive mentality of 'Now I'm going to receive information.' The stand-up meeting is both a discipline—nobody can talk too long, because people get antsy—and a way to get a jump on the morning. We huddle, then someone says 'Break,' and off we go to do our stuff for the day. . . . We try our best to encourage unedited commentary. Otherwise, people start telling you what they think you want to hear."[7]

Do you have a daily routine in place that encourages your team to share unedited commentary on what's going on in their world, as Panner does? Does your morning huddle remind people that your company is based on collaboration, not intimidation? Do members of the team keep their commentary succinct and constructive?

I love this example, because it emphasizes the importance of speed and conciseness in a group setting. Some of the very best training initiatives these days are similarly built to match up with the tight schedules and compressed attention spans of today's workforce. The focus is more and more on bite-sized units of information, rather than days—or even weeks—of training that means sitting passively in a conference room.

Circle K

Circle K is an international chain of over 6,000 convenience stores. One of the company's former executives, Scott Gabriele, was big on capturing Moments of Magic. He instituted a great ritual that supported the team members in his department, making it easy to identify and reinforce the very best things people had accomplished at Circle K. Every Friday, Scott would invite his team into his office for refreshments and a celebration of the successes of the week.

Do you have a weekly routine in place where people can relax and commemorate everything they've achieved? Is your weekly meeting really built around acknowledging what worked—as opposed to pointing fingers and casting blame? If your team gets used to showing up for meetings that are actually about the Failure of the Week, they'll quickly learn to spend most of their time and energy preparing defenses and excuses—no matter what you call the meeting or what refreshments you serve. This is all about getting people together to *celebrate* the week!

Internal Priority: Hire the Attitude—Train the Skill!

Of course, hiring and retention decisions play a critical role in succeeding with this internal commitment. If your organization doesn't yet have in place reliable systems in these areas, then it's time to take a closer look at how you bring people on board, reward them, and develop them over time. As you do so, consider the importance of the *attitude* that a person brings to the table, not just the skills that are on the person's resume. In my opinion, that attitude is the most important thing you are investing in.

As retailer Bruce Nordstrom once said, "We can hire nice people and teach them to sell, but we can't hire salespeople and teach them to be nice." The Nordstrom approach to human resources is worth memorizing and perhaps even framing to hang on your office wall: "Hire the smile . . . train the skill." Someone once noticed that Nordstrom doesn't offer a great deal of formalized training and asked him who trained the staff. The answer: "Their parents."

Once you've got the right team in place, the goal is a pretty simple one: Keep them satisfied by making sure they have great reasons to show up for work in the morning.

> "Opportunity for growth; freedom; the feeling that you are part of something meaningful; feeling valued as a person."
> —Bruce Nordstrom's four reasons people come to work[8]

Please look over Nordstrom's brief but powerful list, and ask yourself this important question: *How many of these reasons are we currently delivering to our team?* If you're feeling really brave, try asking your *team members* the same question.

If you are missing out on even one of those motivators, it's time to make some dramatic changes in the way your organization treats its people. And this chapter has given you some great strategies on how to do just that.

The Keepers

- Remember that the way you treat your employees is your instruction to them on how to treat customers.
- Address employee issues first, before taking on issues with customers.
- You must wow your employees before you can expect them to wow your customers.
- Consider asking team members to contribute, in writing, one idea a week for improvement on any company-related subject of their choosing.
- Consider having weekly team meetings to celebrate what's working. Single out specific employees for public praise when they deliver a great Moment of Magic.
- Consider having brief morning stand-up meetings to review what happened yesterday and what's happening today.
- Hire the attitude, train the skill.

DON'T STOP NOW! In Chapter 10, you'll learn how to use the great internal experience you've created for your team to start building a *process* that doesn't just create loyalty but also encourages *evangelism* with your customers.

Chapter Ten

WHAT THE JOURNEY LOOKS LIKE FROM THE OUTSIDE

THE EXTERNAL MARCH TO *AMAZEMENT*

"You've got to look for a gap, where competitors in a market have grown lazy and lost contact with the readers or the viewers."

—Rupert Murdoch, in response to a question about the key to his success

Let's assume that you've done the internal work that I pointed you toward in Chapter 9. You've laid all the groundwork, gotten the team to a point of true internal alignment with your organization's mission and vision, and you have the right people, in the right jobs, pointed in the right direction. Now what happens on the customer's side of the equation?

This chapter is about the answer to that question. It's an exciting answer, one that I love talking and writing about, and one that I have, in fact, built my whole career around answering. You make the right promise, *and you follow through.* Specifically, you *brand* the experience and bring your customers into *alignment* with that experience. Then, you deliver on the *brand promise*— over and over again. Through this repeated and predictable satisfaction, your customers' confidence increases. Eventually, you develop a network of *evangelists,* who create a community of believers for your organization.

You ultimately find ways to deliver on your promise that consistently exceed customer expectations—and outperform your competitors who are still stuck within the cult of uncertainty. As we've mentioned before, you don't have to deliver wow experiences *all* the time to pull this off, but you do have to deliver a consistently *above-average experience.* When you do this, you point both your organization and its increasingly dedicated community of *evangelists* toward *amazement.*

Consider these examples:

Fall in Love with a Loaf of Bread

Panera Bread is a chain of approximately 1,200 restaurants that is known for its fresh breads, hearty soups, and delicious sandwiches. Their brand promise involves not just great food but human connection as well: "Fresh bread makes friends." And indeed it does. Stop into your local Panera, and you will discover not just bread lovers, but *socializing* bread lovers. Some of them are socializing with friends; others are interacting with family or with business colleagues. And thanks to the chain's popular free wi-fi policy, some are socializing with people half a globe away.

You've got a great thing going when you combine good food with free wi-fi. That's one reason I love Panera so much. This afternoon I was out and I wanted a drink. I could have stopped at a drug store and bought a soda, but I went to Panera. Why? They have free wi-fi. I can relax, have a drink, and check my email. And plus, I bought a muffin. So they got $3.15, and I got a glass of tea, a muffin, and a few minutes of free internet. You can't beat that deal!''—Source: www.ReviewsAndPreviews.blogspot.com

Panera fans fall in love with the *experience* of bread, and connection, at Panera. And they tell their friends about it.

Fall in Love with a Grocery

Wegmans is a Rochester, New York–based supermarket chain that consistently operates within the *cult of amazement*. Wegmans combines an ongoing obsession for food quality and selections with a customer-service experience most shoppers in the United States are still only dreaming about. (Good news—they're expanding.)

Wegmans prides itself on providing an astonishingly wide array of products: 70,000 items in stock per store on average, compared with the industry average of 40,000. Other hallmarks of the Wegmans management style include competitive pricing, listening to customers, placing special orders for them, and (gasp!) making the process of *returning* goods simple and hassle-free. Who do they think they are: Nordstrom? Actually, in a *BusinessWeek* poll a few years back, customers actually rated the Wegmans return-the-merchandise experience *above* Nordstrom's—quite a coup for the Northeastern grocery store chain.

The company's promise is ''Every Day You Get Our Best.'' Coming from another company, that might sound like advertising hokum. But at Wegmans, it really is a way of life. Wegmans boasts stores that are larger than your average grocery store, people who are friendlier than most supermarket employees, and stores *within* the store—such as cafés, cheese shops, pastry shops, and health food shops. The Wegmans experience is addictive, and it's that idea of giving customers the very best that has made the experience possible. Here's what Wegmans has to say about its mission:

> These five statements explain what we're all about:
> 1. We care about and listen to our people.
> 2. High standards are a way of life. We pursue excellence in everything we do.
> 3. We make a difference in every community we serve.
> 4. We respect our people.
> 5. We empower our people to make decisions that improve their work and benefit our customers and our company.[1]

Here are some of the examples of public praise that evangelist shoppers circulate about Wegmans, in return for the company's delivery on those five commitments:

> Is it possible to be obsessed with a grocery store? If you live in the Northeast, you know it is. People who move away miss it; friends and family that come to visit want to go see it. We are four friends who love Wegmans and this blog is where we write about all the things we love most at the store we can't live without.[2]
>
> When we moved to our area, Lehigh Valley PA, the grocery stores really were bad. Fresh produce was awful looking, and selections on other items were slim. Being originally from Upstate NY, I really longed for Wegman's. Finally they made me so happy and built a store here, then another and another! . . . Wegman's still always exceeds my expectations. New products, lots of fresh produce, a great nature's marketplace, and customer service that I adore. I went to one of the local competitors yesterday and could not find anything I was looking for—quick and fresh lunch, kefir in the dairy dept, decent

fruit. Then I went to check out, and the cashier at the self-scan area was plain nasty. I walked my basket to Customer Service set it down and left. Shame on me for going there.[3]

For the uninitiated, Wegmans is the best grocery store ever. If you don't believe me, go to Wegmans on a Friday or Saturday night and try to find a parking space. You won't. It's that popular. They have a regular grocery store setup, with aisles of food (including a good range of international items), but my favorite part is the dining area, possibly because (1) they have delicious food and (2) it looks like Europe (maybe that's just me, but whatever). They have everything from potstickers to ciabatta bread to Angus beef. The mood lighting is in full effect, the ceilings are high and flowerpots behind grated rails hang on Italian stucco-inspired walls. And there's wine in the basement![4]

There are plenty of wow stories from customers who could not believe their luck in finding high-end natural foods on sale at Wegmans—without the high-end prices. Of course, those kinds of wow moments have certainly helped to speed Wegmans and its customers on the journey toward *amazement*. Competitors beware: The family-owned chain is expanding—slowly—so as to ensure that every new Wegmans experience is as *amazing* as the last.

So far, we've seen two examples of companies in alignment with their own brand promises in this chapter—both of which have built strong *communities*, not just customers, and both of which benefit, in a long-term strategic way, from the evangelists in those communities. Now let me tell you a little bit about someone else who has created more than his share of wow moments over the years and attracted legions of evangelists on a scale that most companies can't quite imagine.

A Master of *Amazement*

There is one man who embodies this alignment-to-*amazement* process as impressively as anyone else on the business scene today. He's done the job so well for so long that I'm devoting most of this chapter to him. It's likely that you've heard of him, but I suspect you don't yet really know all you ought to know about him.

The average person probably knows Sir Richard Branson as a flamboyant, risk-taking, jet-setting British business magnate with a penchant for adventure. Some might know that Branson somehow managed to set world records for speed across the Atlantic in a hot air balloon, a sailing vessel, *and* an amphibious craft—and, of course, managed to earn banner headlines along the way with each new record. There have been dozens of similarly masterful public relations stunts, each with Branson's name, picture, and company attached to them. But it's not just Branson's newsworthy and audacious feats that make him especially *amazing*. He has a brilliant mind for business and an uncanny ability to *amaze* his customers.

A Man with a Message

Stepping into the spotlight is something that Branson was apparently born to do, and something he does better than almost any other businessman on earth. *The message* he is reinforcing with each spotlight appearance has a great deal to do with the *cult of amazement*.

There is a common theme to the big adventures: *Richard Branson takes on a tough fight and, against overwhelming odds, gives it everything he has.* That's the story line to most or all of Branson's adventures, and that story line is not an accident. It is an integral part of Branson's corporate branding message.

As it turns out, Branson doesn't just have a gift for adventure; he also has a gift for branding. Put simply, he *lives* his brand—which is, at present, the most dominant in Britain. At the rate he's going, it may well come to be one of the most dominant brands in the world. In fact, Branson's own stated goal is to be as big as Pepsi worldwide during his lifetime.

An April 2007 survey conducted by HPI Research identified Virgin as the single most admired brand in the United Kingdom.

Branson's empire, Virgin Group, currently encompasses holding companies worth over $4 billion. It includes high-profile businesses in media, transportation, tourism, communications, financial services, music, retailing, and publishing. What holds them all together is Branson's own brand promise, which, like his adventures, has something to do with Branson facing overwhelming odds. For him, living the brand is a mission.

Branson's mission drives established competitors crazy. He finds and exploits the weaknesses and oversights of competitors, and he does so in a dramatic fashion that uses his own life story as a powerful marketing and branding tool. He uses this to garner interest and, eventually, loyalty from customers who have become used to what I have called the cult of uncertainty—that inconsistent customer experience delivered by *most* businesses.

Richard Branson *loves* it when an industry is dominated by established companies operating in the cult of uncertainty. He uses this to build a competitive advantage on a consistent, predictable commitment to exceeding customer expectations—in other words, the *cult of amazement.* He almost always does so as a *newcomer* to an industry where so-called major players are delivering uncertainty to their customers. The companies against which Branson competes are usually big—a notion that is important to Branson's story. His competitors typically have one thing in common: They are *bigger* than he is, in the sense that they have more money, more resources, and more customers. But usually, they're not as good as he is at *taking care of* customers.

Branson's brand message—the concept he builds his promise around, the concept he uses to bring consumers (and employees!) into alignment, is this: David versus Goliath.

There are currently over 200 companies under the Virgin umbrella. Every one of those companies somehow touches on the David versus Goliath concept, a concept that Branson himself has repeatedly and explicitly expressed. *Virgin fights the big guys against long odds, and Virgin wins by treating customers better.*

Each Virgin business was founded or acquired under that same basic principle: Let customers know you can deliver a better experience than the big guys can. That's the Virgin message, and that's the Virgin promise.

A Relentless Focus on the Customer Experience

To deliver an experience that's better than what the big guys offer, Branson has built an organization that focuses *relentlessly* on the customer experience, instead of just concentrating on his own company's operating processes. He has developed a company that *listens* to what customers have to say—and does so much more reliably than his competitors. And last but not least, he's created a business that empowers employees to innovate and improve the experience over time, so as to win evangelists and carve out market share.

Branson's commitment to consumers across multiple industries is basically this: "David vs. Goliath means capitalism on your behalf, not the Establishment's." Over the years, Branson has tirelessly maintained countless running story lines that support that promise. The organization's story, like Richard Branson himself, has been simultaneously erratic and predictable, zooming off in a hundred different directions and, at the same time, returning consistently to a single, massive theme that's all but impossible to burn out: David versus Goliath.

The Virgin Group, like the man behind it, is all about taking on established industry players in innovative ways—and consistently delivering a better deal to an underserved consumer that these major players are taking for granted.

Branson himself is refreshingly direct about the story he is telling. "We look to compete with competitors that fit our David to their Goliath image; we look for the big bad wolves that dramatically overcharge and under-deliver."[5] Translation: If you're a big guy who's skimping on or shortchanging customers in any way—watch out!

Consumers and employees alike have fallen in love with that narrative, as has the media. Of course, Branson himself is now one of the big guys, but he's hardly one to let a detail like that get in the way of a good story.

"Virgin stands for value for money, quality, innovation, fun and a sense of competitive challenge." This is the Virgin mantra for the kind of customer experience it aims to deliver across over 200 branded companies.[6]

Telling and Retelling the Story

Because the Branson narrative has been such a critical part of Virgin's success, and because many consumers have only a headline-level familiarity with Virgin, it's important to note a few of the highlights from his extraordinary career. If you really want to understand the challenges that Branson used to confront the big guys—and the high service standards he has introduced in every market in which he competes—you have to take a close look at the way he has mythologized himself and his organization. And I certainly don't use this word in a negative way; creating the right myths or stories is a key to tapping into human emotion, and human emotion is what drives purchasing decisions. I believe every company that gets to the *cult of amazement* must have a *story line*—a myth in the very best sense of that word—that engages and intrigues the customer. Branson's story-line is simple: *I am David, and I will treat you better than Goliath is treating you.*

Study your own marketplace closely, and you will realize that every truly successful organization you are competing against has a story that supports its mantra and its promise. For Branson, *living the brand on a daily basis* is not just a matter of public relations; it's a matter of emotional engagement with the customer! And what better way is there to engage someone's emotions than to tell a great story?

> "Get personally, directly, and emotionally involved in building your brand on a daily basis."
>
> —Richard Branson

The Branson Timeline

1968: Still a teenager attending boarding school, Branson launches an irreverent, cutting-edge magazine entitled *Student* that directly competes with the current youth-oriented publications that he considers out of touch. The magazine is so successful that he decides to drop out of school at the age of 17 so that he can pursue his business interests full-time. Upon Branson's departure from school, the headmaster predicts that he will "end up in prison, or a millionaire."

1971: Branson uses an advertisement in his magazine to launch a successful mail-order record business. That same year, Branson opens a retail record store in London, which he christens Virgin Records and Tapes—a name that plays on the organization's lack of experience. Virgin Records and Tapes caters to a countercultural audience by offering free vegetarian food and beanbag seating for its customers.

1973: Branson decides it's time to launch a record label and builds a recording studio in his home. The first artist he signs is Mike Oldfield, who records the album *Tubular Bells.* This first release is an international hit, sells over five million copies, and provides the theme music for the film *The Exorcist.*

1977: Branson signs a controversial punk-rock band, The Sex Pistols. While other studios are put off by the band's antiestablishment message, Branson thinks they've got something. He's right. The Sex Pistols, according to the BBC, are the "definitive punk rock band. Their controversial songs and live performances are a perfect match for Branson's outrageous personality." The group was another winner for Branson, as Virgin Records becomes one of the leaders in the British music industry.

1979: Branson launches a publishing company that focuses initially on rock music titles that promote the artists Branson has signed to Virgin Records. In 1991, Virgin exploits an underserved community of TV fans by launching a series of books based on the long-canceled, and officially ignored, BBC series *Doctor Who.* The books reach a huge untapped audience and lead to the popular Doctor Who Books imprint.

1984: Branson receives a call from a friend who suggests that he launch a discount transatlantic airline. With no background in aviation beyond his own sense of what a business traveler would like to experience, Branson decides to take on British Airways as a competitor. He appears in a World War I–style flying cap to announce the inaugural flight of Virgin Atlantic. Colleagues and industry insiders predict disaster, but the airline captures the public's imagination and thrives, largely by focusing on improving the perceived quality of the transatlantic flying experience. The airline is honored repeatedly for superior customer service.

1993: Virgin Atlantic archrival British Airways publishes an internally distributed article for its employees that makes profoundly unflattering—and untrue—claims about Branson. Knowing a good PR opportunity when he sees one, Branson sues for libel and eventually receives an out-of-court settlement for over three and half million pounds. He divides the settlement equally among Virgin's staff, and each employee receives just over 160 pounds. Press coverage of the incident is intense and prolonged. Goliath loses to David yet again—in the court of public opinion.

1999: Branson launches the Virgin Mobile cellular phone brand, in partnership with a carefully selected group of telecom providers. The arrangement is an innovative one that uses the networks of other companies and establishes a market niche with pay-as-you-go mobile phone service.

2007: The U.S. airline industry is in turmoil. Industry analysts issue warnings about prolonged downturns and insurmountable competitive challenges. Not surprisingly, Branson chooses this moment to launch Virgin America, and Americans start falling in love with the airline; a love affair is intensifying as this book goes to press.

That same year, Branson teams up with Microsoft co-founder Paul Allen to launch yet another jaw-dropping initiative: Virgin Galactic. The plan is to make zero-gravity flights available to the public by late 2009, making Branson's new enterprise the planet's "first space tourism company specializing in sub-orbital flights to the public." Passengers will be able to unbuckle themselves and float around the cabin for six minutes during the flight. Orbital flights are on the drawing board. The experts are skeptical about his business model, but why should this business be any different than the others?

Don't You Love It When David Beats Goliath?

This is just a sampling of Branson's exploits over the past 40 years. Sure, some of his business ideas didn't work out. Virgin Cosmetics, Virgin Cola, and Virgin Vodka all sputtered out ingloriously, and a high-profile service offering luxury cruise service up and down the Thames was quietly sold to another operator in 2006. However, Branson's successes *far* outweigh his failures, and there is a common pattern in which Richard Branson operates: *He sees an opportunity. He impresses an unhappy or unfulfilled group of customers. Branson beats Goliath.* It's hard not to root for a guy who is always the protagonist in that story line! Every time a customer is exposed to one of his companies, products, or services, or the mediocre service experience a competitor may provide, Branson's David and Goliath brand promise is reinforced.

> "Shape the business around the people."
>
> —Richard Branson

Mission: Find Underwhelmed Customers—and Wow Them!

Richard Branson's story demonstrates one man's efforts to leverage a human personality—his own—to propel a worldwide brand. Branson's approach to capturing market share relies on the promise of a journey to *amazement*—a journey that his competitors have usually neglected to offer. Notice again that *Branson intentionally chooses to compete against companies who have underwhelmed their customers.* He focuses not on his own expertise within a single industry, as many entrepreneurs do, but rather on his own proven ability to shape the business around the people in a way that consistently improves the customer experience and builds loyalty. How does Branson consistently create *amazement?* He focuses on five core values, each of which is a must-have for any enterprise that ends up carrying the Virgin brand.

1. High quality
2. Innovation
3. Good value for the money
4. A challenge to the customers' existing alternatives (the David versus Goliath approach)

5. A need to be fun. If it isn't fun, Branson won't do it. What a way to live! —*Source:* "How Richard Branson Works Magic," *Strategy + Business*, fourth quarter 1998

If any enterprise, idea, product offering, or service offering is missing one of these elements—then Branson wants nothing to do with it!

According to the Virgin Group web site,

When we start a new venture . . . we review the industry and put ourselves in the customer's shoes to see what could make it better. We ask fundamental questions: is this an opportunity for restructuring a market and creating competitive advantage? What are the competitors doing? Is the customer confused or badly served? Is this an opportunity for building the Virgin brand? Can we add value? Will it interact with our other businesses? Is there an appropriate trade-off between risk and reward?

Branson himself puts the matter somewhat more concisely—and memorably: Starting up a business "is done on gut feeling—especially if I can see that they are taking the *mickey* out of the consumer." That's British slang. "Taking the mickey out of the customer," roughly translated, means having a joke at the customer's expense. Think of the mickey as taking advantage of the customer, or not giving good value for the money. Branson's obsession with the subject of taking better care of customers eventually earned him a knighthood. In 1999, he became Sir Richard Branson for his "services to entrepreneurship."

Five Critical Pathways

Virgin's remarkable story proves that customers will sign up for your organization's journey out of uncertainty, based on five critical factors that are similar to the internal experience facets covered in Chapter 9:

- *Little things that mean a lot.* What personal messages are we sending the customer about how much we value the relationship? Branson pays attention to details. For example, many of the amenities that are considered extraordinary on most major airlines are the norm on Virgin Air. For example, Virgin provides both scheduled *and* on-demand movie service—in coach! That's in addition to the ample selections available on Virgin's free satellite TV service, of course. If you get tired of all that, you can start a text-chat room with other passengers on the flight! As of this writing, Virgin is working on giving you access to e-mail during your flight. Other airlines may be working on this, but don't bet against Branson doing it first—and perhaps finding a way to offer it for free.
- *Problem solving and recovery.* Do we turn Moments of Misery into Moments of Magic? A captain on a Virgin America flight, rather than making an announcement over the loudspeaker system, actually left the cockpit to personally tell the passengers why they were going to be delayed. Imagine that!
- *Opportunity knocks.* Are we willing to improve on an average experience, without the customer having to ask for it? Anyone who has flown a Virgin flight has experienced this in one way or another. Upper-class passengers, for instance, are regularly *reminded* by the flight crew that the price of their journey includes amenities like acupuncture and manicure services! The folks in coach are likely to get similar reminders from the staff about the massive library of video games available.
- *Proactive culture.* Do we anticipate customer needs and problems—and address them as early as possible? This may be the key to Virgin's success. They look for the opportunities that other companies have missed or neglected. How many

airlines offer you a sleeping blindfold and a fresh pair of socks for overnight trips? No, you don't have to fly upper-class to get these free of charge.

- *The Art of Wow.* Do we deliver experiences that make customers stop and think, "That's *amazing*"? Branson's whole career has been built around the idea of identifying and executing wow-level Moments of Magic! The best current example is Branson's Virgin Galactic initiative, where he plans to make going into outer space available to the public. As big as that may sound, you can bet he's on the lookout for an even bigger wow to deliver to his customers—and the global audience he's enthralled for decades with new variations on his David versus Goliath story.

What's Your Message?

If Branson's message is "David taking on Goliath—on your behalf!"—what's *your* message to customers? What's your *promise?* How can you define it—and keep it—as a member of

- The Force of One?
- The Force Within?
- The Force of Many?

The answers await you in Chapter 11.

The Keepers

- Know your promise to the consumer—and deliver on it, no matter what. (Examples: "Fresh bread makes friends." "Every day, you get our best." "I'm David, taking on Goliath on your behalf.")
- Know the story—the mythology—that supports your brand promise.

- Live your brand!
- Find underwhelmed consumers and wow them.
- Remember Sir Richard Branson's five prerequisites: high quality, innovation, value for money, challenging existing alternatives, and fun.
- Follow Branson's advice: Shape the business around the people.

Chapter Eleven

LAUNCHING THE *AMAZEMENT REVOLUTION*

So now what?

If you've made it this far in the book, I'm hoping that you're now motivated to move your customers, yourself, your department, or your entire organization toward the *cult of amazement*. This is where customers get so used to the experience of *consistently* receiving above-average service that they start singing your praises to the world and recruiting other customers on your behalf. They literally become evangelists for you and your company.

As we have seen, most organizations do not operate within this cult. Most operate simply by default within the cult of uncertainty, where neither the customers nor the employees are aligned with any guiding vision or brand promise and the experience is inconsistent, both internally and externally. People simply don't know what to expect.

Maybe your organization is stuck in uncertainty, or maybe you're navigating through one of the other cults: alignment, experience, ownership, or ultimately, *amazement*. Regardless of where you currently are, you now represent one of three possible forces that are all in motion toward the *cult of amazement*. Take a look at the brief list that follows, and see which category best describes your current situation.

Three Forces for *Amazement*

I am a Force of One. I am the only person who ever has direct contact with my customers. At the end of the day, I—and I alone—control all aspects of my customers' experience with my business.

I am part of a Force Within. I work within a larger organizational structure that is, as a whole, stuck in a cult other than *amazement* (typically uncertainty). However, I myself am committed to delivering above-average experiences to both internal and external customers.

I am part of a Force of Many. I lead or work within a larger organizational structure that has moved past uncertainty and into at least alignment. The organization has leadership that is eager to move forward into *amazement,* both internally and externally, and all employees are on board with that goal.

Take note: You can be currently *operating* at the *cult of amazement* and at the same time still be *striving* for *amazement.* This may seem like a contradiction, but it's not. It is, in fact, a necessary process; people don't simply decide to operate within *amazement* and immediately find themselves there. It takes work and progress. Getting into the *cult of amazement* is good, but staying there is what makes you great—and creates customer evangelists.

Touch Points and Impact Points

To launch an *amazement* revolution in your world, you must take control of two very important things: *touch points* and *impact points.* They are interrelated aspects you must focus on equally. Concentrating only on one or the other is a habit of organizations that operate in uncertainty.

Let's define touch points first. Each and every time we interact with a customer, we have the opportunity to make an impression that can make or break the customer relationship. These touch points can be face-to-face meetings, conversations over the phone, or even Internet and web site interactions, but they have in common the fact that they all operate on the front line.

Former president of Scandinavian Airlines Jan Carlzon calls these interactions Moments of Truth, and he wrote a great business book by the same name. Carlzon's book explains how he rescued his troubled airline by improving on clearly identified Moments of Truth. The book was a big inspiration for me when it first came out and a major reason why I went into the business of working with organizations to improve the impressions they create with customers. Here is the critical strategy Carlzon used to launch what I would call an amazement revolution within Scandinavian Airlines:

> "Any time a customer comes into contact with any aspect of your business—however remote—they have an opportunity to form an impression."
>
> —Jan Carlzon[1]

Carlzon worked from that principle and identified a list of the Moments of Truth that the passenger experienced on Scandinavian Airlines—and promptly shared them with every employee in the organization. The result was one of the great turnarounds in business history. Not only did Scandinavian Airlines become successful again but also it became the most admired airline in the industry!

Carlzon's list of critical Moments of Truth for the airline's passengers included:

- Making a reservation
- Picking up the ticket at the city ticket office

- Checking the bags curbside on the day of departure
- Checking in at the ticket counter
- Boarding the plane
- Receiving any kind of service from flight personnel during the flight
- Being greeted at the destination
- Picking up bags at the baggage claim area

Carlzon realized that these Moments of Truth were the critical interactions that would influence a passenger's decision about what kind of airline he or she was flying on. Such moments aren't unique to Scandinavian Airlines; they are, for any airline, the moments when a passenger forms an enduring impression. And there are also less obvious Moments of Truth. For example, assume that you're a passenger walking toward your boarding gate, and an employee from the airline smiles at you. As inconsequential as that interaction may seem, it is nevertheless an important Moment of Truth. A smile from an airline employee elevates the average or mundane experience to something just a little bit better than average; it even goes so far as to create a sense of comfort for a nervous flier. Even the small touch points are important!

Think of touch points as the *chain of events* that the customer experiences, with each item on the list being a link in the chain. Every business—every organization—has touch points.

Every business also has *impact points,* which are the series of events that occur behind the scenes. Though customers may never actually see an impact point—or even know that one exists or how one works—these out-of-sight moments always affect them in one way or another.

Imagine, for example, that you're checking in for your flight, and you hand your bags to the person at the ticket counter. That is a touch point, but once the bags are out of sight, the impact points take over. Those bags don't just show up at your destination magically. There is a procedure—and a number of people involved in following it—in place. This process and these people ensure that your bags arrive at your destination at the same time that you do. The people behind the scenes may never have face-to-face interaction with the customer, but their responsibilities *definitely* have an impact on the passenger!

Think of impact points—just like touch points—as *links in a chain.* These long series of actions guide the airline's internal processes and may actually end up driving the customer's overall service experience. Impact points are mostly or completely in-visible to customers; in fact, if an impact point is well designed and links seamlessly with other impact points, then they *should* be virtually invisible to the customer. If they become visible, it's because a process has broken down somewhere along the line.

For instance, imagine that you show up at the baggage carou-sel to claim your bag but end up having to wait for over an hour. If something that should ideally take only a few minutes ends up taking that long, it's likely that the system—or the chain—experienced a setback somewhere. There was a weak link in the chain of impact points.

Now suppose that after an hour-long wait for your bags, you decided to go to the baggage claims desk for help and encoun-tered an airline employee who seemed indifferent to your situa-tion. That's a touch point going wrong.

It is the combination of frontline touch points and behind-the-scenes impact points that creates the service experience. If you are planning to launch an *amazement revolution,* I hope you can see how essential it is to understand both the touch points and the impact points in your organization.

> "What we need are more people who specialize in the impossible."
>
> —Theodore Roethke

Those of us who are lucky enough to be on the inside of an organization that is aligned with and moving toward *amazement* must constantly look for ways to improve both touch points and impact points; it is an ongoing mission. If you recall Don Wainwright's emphasis on building a culture that makes continuous improvements to its own processes—and Richard Branson's insistence on listening to customers and persistently (re)building businesses around them—then you have some idea of the importance of this mission.

If you are launching an *amazement revolution*, you must look for ways to upgrade and improve both touch points and impact points on a regular basis. You simply cannot launch an *amazement revolution* if you are ever the least bit complacent about the job of improving these aspects of your business. You must be willing to reexamine them continually in the light of new customer feedback, changes in the marketplace, and the latest technology.

> *Believe it!* Companies that have worked their way forward to the *cult of amazement* must continually refine and upgrade their touch points and impact points if they plan to *stay* in the *cult of amazement*.

Remember: touch points and impact points are interrelated. If your organization uses impact points to support some, most, or all of the touch points you deliver to customers, then you cannot simply demand that your employees start upgrading the *quality* of the customer experience without first improving the internal impact points they are using. *Touch points and impact points must be improved simultaneously!* Everyone who is involved with any type of impact point connects to the customer in an indirect way. Even those who don't have direct contact with a customer are likely to be supporting—or being supported by—someone who does. Therefore, by the same logic, you must also manage the touch points your internal customers experience—in addition to managing any impact points of which you may be a part of.

Are You Operations-Focused or Customer-Focused?

From the customer's point of view, a single Moment of Truth can define an entire organization.

Think about that for a moment: *One* interaction with an employee who is having a bad day, who has been improperly trained, or who has been placed in the wrong position may distinguish the entire customer experience and, potentially, the entire company. At any given time, one person will represent the entire organization: the brand, the other employees, the building, everything. Every employee must know and understand the importance of this inescapable reality, which I call the *awesome responsibility.*

To get a sense of this concept, imagine that you're a guest at a hotel taking the elevator up to your room. As the elevator doors open, you notice that a maintenance man has placed a ladder directly in front of the elevator doors and is now balanced on it, working intently on something above the elevator door. It's a very minor inconvenience. The worker is oblivious to you, and he continues concentrating on his current task as you squeeze by the ladder. He doesn't say a word to you. As you make your way down the hall, you think to yourself, "The people at this hotel certainly aren't very friendly."

Now rewind that same scenario and play it back—with a twist. You're getting ready to step out of the elevator. When the doors open, you notice that there's a ladder in front of you. As you squeeze by, the workman above you looks down with a smile and says, "Hello!" Maybe he asks you what kind of day you've had or where you're from. As you make your way toward your room, you think to yourself, "What a great choice this hotel was. The people here are so friendly!" And you don't even notice that the ladder was in the way.

Notice that in both of these stories you thought that the *people* were either friendly or not so friendly. It wasn't the *people,* it was the *person.* A single employee made an impression for the entire hotel and its staff, hence the awesome responsibility.

The key to fulfilling the awesome responsibility of representing the organization to the world is to be consistently *customer-focused*, as was the worker in the second example. Yet one of the most common preventable causes of a Moment of Misery is the decision to focus on our organization's *process*, rather than on the customer.

I have several clients in the health care industry who place a huge emphasis on customer (that is, patient) service. Unfortunately, these organizations have been facing a nurse shortage in recent times. The nurses they interview must meet certain educational requirements to become licensed or certified. Although many of these people have all of the technical skills and knowledge to be proficient nurses, a good number of them do *not* have the people skills to deliver the level of service the hospital wants to provide to their patients and their families.

So, what should the hiring managers do? Is it better to hire someone with all the technical skills who is low on warmth, empathy, and conversational ability? From an operations perspective, everything is in place. But from a customer perspective, there's a challenge. The hospital doesn't simply want to hire skilled nurses; they want to hire skilled nurses who are also *customer-focused.*

Do you see the challenge here? Although the nurse may be great at drawing blood, dispensing medications, and performing all the other operational aspects of the job, that same nurse may not be very good at an equally critical part of the job—namely, being nice to the patient! This presents a significant challenge to the customer-centered manner of doing business.

The Disney organization is an excellent example of a customer-centric institution. They always begin by hiring the right person for the job. Before the employees (known as cast members within the organization) ever begin their assigned jobs, they go through some basic training, which Disney refers to as traditions. This process grants the new staff members an understanding of how to manage the magic at Disney. Instead of training these new cast members on the jobs they were hired to do, most of this training is focused instead on interactions with guests. Walt Disney used to tell his Disneyland cast members that they had *three* jobs: doing whatever it was they had been hired to do, taking care of the guest, and keeping the park clean. (And I get the feeling that keeping the park clean was part of the larger mission of ensuring that the customer always felt welcome and comfortable at Disneyland!)

> "Give the public everything you can give them, keep the place as clean as you can keep it, and keep it friendly."
>
> —Walt Disney

If you really want to launch an *amazement revolution*, you must accept that you and your employees have two jobs: to do what they are hired to do *and* to do *everything* and *anything* necessary to take care of the customer. (Keeping the place clean is a bonus!) You must create—and constantly *re-create*—a customer-focused organization. Anything less places you and your organization indefinitely in the cult of uncertainty.

Five Human Resource Strategies You Must Implement on the Inside if You Plan to Build a Customer-Focused Organization

1. Hire right, and make sure you have the right person for the job. When in doubt, hire on attitude—and train the technical skills later. The fact that someone has great technical skills does *not* mean the person should be interacting with customers most of the day.
2. Train constantly. This means training in both technical skills and soft skills such as customer service and communication skills.
3. Recognize individual successes. When people get things right, offer them authentic public and private praise.

(continued)

(*continued*)

4. Celebrate team successes. Think of reasons to celebrate when the team achieves certain goals.

5. Treat your employees the way you want your customers treated—maybe even better. Yes, I'm repeating this—that's how very important it is. I have yet to run into an organization that couldn't benefit from having this message repeated on a regular basis.

Six Exercises That Will, Step by Step, Help You Start an *Amazement Revolution*

The five strategies just outlined are focused on human resource issues: hiring, training, employee relations, and so forth. What follows are six specific exercises that you need to complete to begin your journey toward *amazement*. Please bear in mind that these exercises—like everything else I can share with you about the journey to *amazement*—are just part of the process of an *ongoing* mission. If you are now in uncertainty, you still need to work your way through alignment, ownership, and experience before you get to the *cult of amazement*, and even once you make it to *amazement*, you will have to work to remain there. All of this takes time and persistence, and the exercises listed next will help you through the process of taking all of these concepts to your *outside* customers.

1. Make an effort to identify every touch point that you and your company have with your customers. Think of these as the chain of events that a typical customer encounters. You may have several of these chains, depending on the different ways or reasons a customer has for interacting with you.

2. Next, identify the touch points that are the strongest opportunities to turn a one-time customer into a repeat customer.

3. Look for the weakest links in the chain; in other words, look for the touch points that could possibly turn into Moments of Misery. Once you've identified them, determine what you can do to strengthen them and turn them into Moments of Magic.

4. Next, recognize all the behind-the-scene impact points that support—or *could* support—those touch points. It is very likely that you will need to create *chains* of impact points, like the chain of events you created for the customer's touch points.

5. Then—as you identified the weak links in the chain of touch points—look for weak links with the impact points that could cause a breakdown in the process or system. Brainstorm on how to avoid these problems and eliminate the weak links.

6. Commit your list of touch points and supporting impact points to writing, and review them at least once a month with everyone in your organization. If you see something that could be improved—and you almost certainly will— take the initiative and improve it.

If You Are Operating as a Force of One . . .

Complete the six exercises, and make doing so an integral and ongoing part of your business. You are fortunate to have the easiest possible path when it comes to launching an *amazement revolution*; unlike those operating in the Force Within and the Force of Many, you—and you alone—have total control of the customer experience. You can personally change any process that isn't working without having to get approval from anyone.

If You Are Operating as a Force Within . . .

Share this book with your colleagues, especially those in leadership positions. Ask which ideas and principles seem most relevant to your organization. Try to enlist management into beginning the journey to *amazement*. Do your best, using the time and resources available to you, to identify the most critical touch points and impact points in your world. The six exercises will give you a good start.

Record what you know *ought* to happen if your company were operating in the *cult of amazement*. Show how regulation of the relevant touch points and impact points could positively affect employees and customers. Write down—in easily understandable words and steps—*exactly* what makes it possible for you to deliver the Moments of Magic to both internal *and* external customers. At the very least, you can use this work to support smooth transitions when people are trained to take over new positions in your area or if a situation arises when someone must fill in for you on short notice.

Finally, keep an eye out for *amazement allies*. These are people with whom you may work closely, or perhaps those in other departments, who are on the same page with you and who share your commitment to providing a stellar customer experience and moving customers out of uncertainty and toward *amazement*. Your formal or informal contacts with these allies will help you keep your perspective—and even your sanity—when things get bumpy. *Amazement* allies can become your support system in solving customer and internal issues. Know whom to go to and whom you can count on. Interact, converse, and network with these allies to spread the *amazement revolution*. If you're lucky, your *amazement* ally will be someone like the CEO of your company. And if you're *really* lucky, that CEO will have read this book!

If You Are a Leader of a Company That Has a Force Within . . .

Beware! You are in a vulnerable position. You have one or more islands of employees operating as Forces Within. That means your organization is at grave competitive risk for the following reasons:

- The people who know best how to deliver Moments of Magic—those who are working as a Force Within—may not have enough support and may soon burn out.
- These same people, who are the very best you have, may be recruited by the competition.
- Because of lack of support or burnout, the members of these Forces Within may simply decide to stop trying.
- Because of the employees who aren't part of the Force Within, the organization is at great risk of delivering an inconsistent experience to internal and external customers. (In fact, it's not a risk—it's a certainty!)

Sometimes a leader may hear that customers are asking—specifically and repeatedly—to work with a particular employee. If your company is not yet operating within the *cult of amazement,* this is your clue that there *is* a Force Within and, at the same time, that your company may be delivering an inconsistent customer experience. Why are the customers asking for that specific employee rather than anyone else? Is it because they have had a less than stellar experience with another employee? Is this person the only employee customers trust? What is this person doing that other people in your organization should be doing? The answer to that question may point you toward some of your best strategies for expanding the Force Within—and moving toward a Force of Many.

If You Are Operating as a Force of Many . . .

Remember that everything you have read in this chapter applies to you and your organization. Even if all of your employees are operating at the level of *amazement,* new hires, lack of training, complacency, and other issues can detract from your customer experience vision.

You may be interested to learn that many of my best clients are companies who already operate in the *cult of amazement* and already get this but understand how easy it is to lose their competitive advantage. When your customer has learned to expect the best, it's all too easy to fall from grace! Even though you dwell in the *cult of amazement* now, you are just one under-trained employee, one harsh word, or one Moment of Misery away from the customer saying, "They're slipping! Let's take a look at the competition."

The good news about being in the *cult of amazement* is that if there is a Moment of Misery, many of your customers will have confidence in you to fix the problem. Operating in the *cult of amazement* earns you the right to stay in the game and gives you the chance to redeem yourself and your company. Make the most of that opportunity by always being prepared to tweak what's working and find ways to make it work better and by constantly striving for improvement. Remain open to hearing about things that aren't working, and find ways to fix them. Make sure you give recognition to the employees who bring problems and customer issues to your attention.

Don't rest on your laurels. Make sure that your entire team not only is in alignment *today* but also *stays* in alignment tomorrow. This requires constant alignment training from both internal and external sources, as well as a stream of never-ending daily remind-ers from the top company players about the principles that drive your commitments to both employees and customers. In the end, the *cult of amazement* is always maintained by supporting, building, and repairing relationships. If your organization ever falls out of the habit of improving relationships with its customers and employees, you will quickly drop out of alignment and slip back into the cult of uncertainty. That's definitely *not* where you, your people, or your customers want to be.

Remember always that *amazement* is a journey, not a destina-tion. You must commit yourself and your organization to *continu-ous evaluation and improvement* of the touch points and impact points that connect you to your customers!

The Keepers

- Touch points are the frontline interactions that customers have with your company and employees.
- Impact points happen inside the company and should remain invisible to the external customer. Despite their behind-the-scenes nature, they have a direct impact on the external customer's experience.
- You cannot focus only on touch points if you hope to make the journey to *amazement*. You must be equally focused on the impact points that support the touch points in order to have direct impact on the customer.
- When impact points are well designed and link seamlessly, they support positive customer experiences—ideally, Moments of Magic.
- Even if you are not directly supporting a customer, you are most likely to be involved in a process that does. Manage the touch points that you have with internal customers.
- We each carry an *awesome responsibility*—because at any given time, the one person with whom the customer is interacting can define the organization as a whole.
- If you have a consistent *customer* focus, you are operating in or moving toward the *cult of amazement*. If you have a consistent *operations* focus with your external customers, you are probably operating in the cult of uncertainty.
- Implement these five strategies to help build a customer-focused organization: (1) Hire right, (2) train constantly in both hard technical skills and soft customer-service skills, (3) recognize individual success, (4) celebrate team accomplishments, and (5) treat your employees the way you want your customers treated—maybe even better.
- If you're operating as a Force of One, take the time to document and refine the touch points and impact points that allow you to deliver Moments of Magic.

- If you're operating as part of a Force Within, share the concepts in this book with your leadership, and keep an eye out for *amazement* allies.
- If you're already lucky enough to be operating as part of a Force of Many, remember that *amazement* is a continuous journey, not a destination.

Part Four

AMAZEMENT IN ACTION

The next five chapters give you dozens of real-life examples of companies who've managed to create Moments of Magic. Think of these as miniature case studies that show how these groups move customers and employees along the path toward the cult of amazement. The snapshots this part offers of above-average internal and external customer experiences feature examples from the following categories:

Chapter 12: Little Things—experiences that require only modest investments of time and energy but can have a big impact.

Chapter 13: Problem Solving and Recovery—experiences that show how Moments of Misery can quickly turn into Moments of Magic.

Chapter 14: Opportunity Knocks—experiences that prove your organization is ready and willing to improve on a fair, average, or acceptable experience—without anyone having to ask for it.

Chapter 15: Proactive Service and Follow-Through—experiences that prove you should anticipate needs and problems—and address them early.

Chapter 16: The Art of Wow—amazing, truly memorable positive experiences that win attention and respect, raise the bar, and turn satisfied customers into customer evangelists!

Many of these examples are from my own personal encounters, and some are stories I've read or heard about from others. I come across a lot of examples of above-average service in my line of business, in part because I work with some great companies that are eager to turn their customers into evangelists and also because I travel a great deal. I am therefore exposed to countless companies I hope will deliver a service experience that you find in the cult of amazement.

The best of the stories I've gathered over the years are recorded here. Of course, not every example offers specifics that apply to your company, your industry, or your personal situation. However, you can learn from all of them. Each of the snapshots in this part features a lesson that offers potential relevance to *everyone* who reads this book.

Browse through the stories, and see which ones resonate with your current personal and professional position. Think about how the *lesson* behind an incident might apply to your situation, even if the specific company or industry portrayed doesn't. Try to find a half-dozen or so lessons that you could start implementing in your organization . . . today!

Even if all you get from this section (or this entire book) is a *single* idea that you can execute consistently, your payback will be exponentially higher than the price of this book!

Chapter Twelve

LITTLE THINGS

SNAPSHOTS OF ORGANIZATIONS AND PEOPLE WHO GET THE LITTLE THINGS RIGHT

Our perceptions of the organizations with which we choose to work are inevitably shaped by a sequence of seemingly little experiences that can go either well or poorly. Take a look at these examples of companies that made a big positive impression by focusing on the small stuff.

Sweet!

When guests sit down for dinner at the Italian chain restaurant Brio, they might not be consciously aware that the colored sugar packets at their table are carefully arranged with exactly 12 pink packets, 12 yellow packets, and 12 white packets of sugar. Every time a staff member prepares a table for a new guest, no more and no less than 12 sugar packets for each color are placed in the little sugar containers. Although this may seem like a ridiculous detail to manage, it is not; it is but one example of how important it is to manage *all* of the details of presentation. This attention to specifics sends a subliminal message of order and implies a sense of care for the customer—which helps to ensure that his or her experience is top-notch. In a similar way, Jan Carlzon—the breakthrough leader I discussed in Chapter 11—made an important point about the customer experience to his employees at Scandinavian Airlines. Carlzon emphasized that small details *do* make a difference. For example, a passenger who takes a seat on a Scandinavian Airlines flight and pulls down the tray table to see a coffee stain might draw negative assumptions about the entire airline. Carlzon recognized that *failing* to execute on the little things can send potentially disastrous messages to customers. When the airline doesn't wipe down the tray tables, they may be sending a false message about how they service the engines. When the restaurant doesn't replenish the sugar and instead leaves crumpled, unsorted sugar containers in the bowl, they may be sending a false message about the hygiene standards in the kitchen!

LESSON ONE: Part of a great service experience is in the details. Sometimes those details are almost invisible and may appear to go unnoticed, but they are the little things that help drive the quality experience.

LESSON TWO: Not managing even the smallest details can send false messages about much bigger issues to your customers.

Stay in Touch

Because a number of my clients are in the financial services industry, I've noticed an interesting commonality among top sales performers in this line of work: They're usually very good at keeping in touch with their clients and prospects. They're always finding a reason to check in by phone, send an e-mail, or pass along an article. It might be for a birthday, holiday, or anniversary; any event, big or small, can serve as an excuse to reach out to the people for whom they provide service. These little contacts improve the customer's relationship and experience with the salesperson and the organization.

There is no reason for not using this practice in virtually *every* industry. It is simply an excuse to put your name in front of your customer, and it works for employees as well! A thank-you note, holiday card, or congratulatory message shows that you are thinking of your employees.

LESSON: Reach out to your customers and employees, just to let them know you are thinking of them.

Thank-You Notes and Follow-Up

Not long ago, I bought some clothes at my local Neiman Marcus. Several days later, I was opening my mail and found a personalized note from the salesperson who had served me, thanking me for my purchase. Two months later, the salesperson sent me a postcard announcing an upcoming sale. Several months after that, I got a voice-mail message from the salesperson telling me about another sale.

This guy knew exactly what he was doing! Maybe he had programmed some piece of software with all the names of his customers to issue reminders to keep in touch on a regular basis, or maybe he just had an old-fashioned address book. Whatever it was, it worked. I'm now a regular at that store, and I always enjoy seeing *my guy*.

LESSON: Set up a system that keeps information on your customers and employees and helps you stay in touch on a regular basis.

Get the E-Mail Address!

Many people are afraid to give out their e-mail address, and rightly so. All of the junk e-mail that comes in as a result can be a big inconvenience. However, if you create a good experience for customers, they will gladly give you their e-mail addresses. They want you to keep in touch, and they want you to tell them how they can keep those good experiences coming!

My wife and I recently tried a new restaurant in our town, and we were very pleased with the experience. On our way out, the hostess thanked us and asked for our e-mail address. If a total stranger had asked us for this information, we would have gone into spam-prevention mode and immediately refused, but the fact that our pleasant hostess was asking us—and was doing so after we'd had a great meal—made it easy for us to give her the information.

Two days later, we received an e-mail thanking us for our business and telling us about a special promotion we could take advantage of the next time we came in. Every month, we receive an e-mail with the newest specials. (That's about the right frequency, by the way; you don't want to bombard people with marketing e-mail.) Since then, we've gone back several times—and we've always enjoyed our meals there.

LESSON: Right after a customer has a positive experience is the best time to ask for an e-mail address. Once you have it, use it effectively and respectfully. Don't abuse the privilege of having the e-mail address by overcommunicating.

Getting It Down in Black and White

Glen Brown, the former CEO of a trucking company out of Joplin, Missouri, used to write a short note at least twice a year to each and every one of the thousand-plus employees in his company. Sometimes he would send a holiday or birthday card;

other times, it was a congratulatory note of some kind. Sometimes the messages were more generic. Regardless, every one of his colleagues was touched at least twice a year.

These messages showed employees that Glen cared. They kept him in touch with everyone in the company, even the truckers who seldom came into the office. This earned Glen a tremendous amount of respect and admiration from his employees and showed him to be a true leader.

LESSON: Send personalized communications to your internal team. It shows that you care and sets an excellent example of how you want other employees—as well as customers—treated.

The Valet and the Bentley

Scott was a special hotel doorman.

One day a guest arrived at the beautiful Ritz-Carlton Hotel in St. Louis. He was driving a rental car, and he was having some trouble getting out of it. The guest couldn't seem to find the door handle right away. Scott opened the man's car door for him from the outside and welcomed him to the hotel. The man jokingly complained that he should have found a better rental car. Tongue in cheek, Scott joked back and told the guest he would try to find a Bentley for him before he left. That humor and special attention earned Scott a *hundred-dollar* tip from this customer.

In fact, Scott received a *series* of fat tips from this gentleman, all of which had resulted from Scott's willingness to start a conversation on the customer's terms and keep coming back to that conversation. The "I'll get you a Bentley" exchange quickly became a running joke between the two. Before the guest left the hotel, Scott gave him a small model Bentley!

The $60 Scott shelled out for that tiny Bentley was not much compared with the several hundred dollars in tips that he received from this guest, but that's really not the point. The point is that Scott loves people. He engages them in conversation and loves the interaction.[*]

LESSON: Being approachable enhances the customer experience. Being conversational, at the right times, takes it to a higher level.

There's Magic in a Name

A while back, I had the good fortune to work at the Morton's Steakhouse managers' meeting at the Four Seasons resort on the beautiful island of Nevis. The moment I stepped off the plane, I spotted a sign with my name on it, carried by a representative from the travel company that was managing the conference. She approached me and asked, "How was your flight, Mr. Hyken?" I told her it had been fine. She smiled and arranged for my cab.

She must have given the cabdriver my name because he asked, "Where are you from, Mr. Hyken?" We had a nice little chat.

When we finally arrived at the resort, the doorman said, "Welcome to our hotel, Mr. Hyken." Someone must have told him I was on my way. (I bet it was the person who met me at the airport.) The woman at the front desk didn't ask my name; she already knew it! She said, "Checking in, Mr. Hyken?" Wow!

The bellhop used my name, too, as we were walking up to my room. This was *amazing*! Later in the day, I ran into the housekeeper—who greeted me by name and asked whether she was pronouncing it properly! Throughout the entire stay, the staff at the Four Seasons greeted me by name.

It may take a little time and effort to learn the names and faces of your customers, but it's worth it. Your goal is to give a customer a memorable experience. Using someone's name is

---

[*]To learn more about Scott Ginsberg, a truly remarkable guy, a talented author, and the nation's premier expert on approachability, visit www .HelloMyNameIsScott.com.

special and personal, and it definitely adds to the customer's experience.

LESSON: Take the time and effort to learn your customer's name and use it. Dale Carnegie once said, "Remember that a man's name, to him, is the sweetest and most important sound in any language."

Hospitals Can Say Thank You, Too

Not long ago, my wife had minor surgery. Just three days after the surgery—which was a complete success—she received a thank-you card from the hospital. The card came signed by Phyllis Austin, Director of Surgical Services, and it thanked her for choosing Missouri Baptist Medical Center. The card also included hand-written notes from two of the nurses and wishes for a quick recovery from several people on her OR team.

In today's competitive business marketplace, even hospitals have to compete for business in a way that's never been necessary before, and Missouri Baptist Medical Center gets this. I was particularly impressed with this gesture, because it supported a larger culture of the *people-first* type of patient care at that institution. To quote the Robin Williams character Patch Adams in the film with the same name: "You treat a disease; you win, you lose. You treat a person; I'll guarantee you'll win."

LESSON ONE: Thank-you notes are powerful. Use them.

LESSON TWO: The human side of business is almost always more important than the operations side.

The Paint Cup Crew

Last year I saw something that inspired me to improve my own business.

I was in a building and noticed two maintenance workers walking down the hall and inspecting the walls and baseboards carefully. Each was armed with a small paintbrush and a cup of paint. One was carrying a cup of white paint, and the other, a cup of gray paint. I watched them for a few minutes and concluded that their job was to go through the building, search out nicks and chips, and then touch up those spots with paint.

And what a difference they made. The hallway looked super-sharp after they left the premises.

I started thinking about the little nicks and scratches I could start touching up for my customers. Maybe every organization needs the equivalent of a paint cup crew: someone whose assignment it is to wander around purposefully and fix up the minor blemishes, nicks, and scratches that inevitably become noticeable.

LESSON: Keep an eye out for the little touch-ups you can do that will have a big impact on your customer's world.

Anti-No

I was out for dinner with some friends recently when the server suggested we split some appetizers, one of which was a shrimp dish with three large barbecued shrimp. One of my friends said, "There are four of us. If we paid extra, do you think you could put another shrimp on the plate?"

The server smiled and said, "We're a 'don't-like-to-say-no' kind of restaurant. Of course we can put an extra shrimp on the dish for you."

John DiJulius, author of *What's the Secret?* and a good friend of mine, writes about his client, Cameron Mitchell restaurants, and their brand promise: "The answer is yes; now what's the question?"

Another great example of the anti-no philosophy comes from the retailer Neiman Marcus. Not long ago, I bought a pair of pants there. I asked my sales rep, Patty, whether the pants would shrink if they were washed at home. Patty didn't give me any details about the warranty or the store's policy. Instead, she simply made a promise that made my experience at Neiman Marcus a complete *yes* experience: "If there is anything wrong with the pants after you wash them ten times," she said, "just bring them back." No conditions, no loopholes, no excuses—nothing but *yes!*

LESSON: Ask yourself: Are you a don't-like-to-say-no kind of organization? What would it take for you to become one?

Care More about the Customer Than You Do about the Business

Writer Mark Vittert of the *St. Louis Business Journal* pens a regular column titled *Reflections.* I'm a big fan of Mark's; his column is always the first part of the paper I read. One piece in particular stood out to me as a keeper. Mark wrote about Irv Roselman, an insurance salesperson for Lincoln Life. He described how his father had purchased a small policy from Irv over 50 years ago. After closing that initial policy, Irv never made another sale to the Vittert family. Yet over the course of five decades, Irv found a reason to stay in touch with the family. He first corresponded with Mark's father and then with Mark himself. Mark would receive a card on his birthday, and sometimes Irv would write a nice note when he heard a piece of news connected to Mark's family.

There is a great business lesson here about staying in touch simply for the sake of staying in touch. Sending cards for 50 years—despite never making another sale—shows that Irv cared more about his clients than he did about making the sale. Irv remained loyal to his customers. It didn't matter to him whether people bought another policy from him; he would still keep in touch. That's just the way Irv was.

LESSON: Prove to your clients that you are more interested in them than you are in the sale. This may—or may not—lead to more business, but it will definitely help the relationship, which is a big part of building customer loyalty.

The Bottom Line

The little things you do to make the customer's experience better have *big* impact. Manage the details. Use small touches, like the ones you've read about in this chapter, to show customers and employees that you care about what happens in their world. If you make a consistent commitment to deliver on these little experiences, you will generate huge loyalty, and huge paybacks on the investment, over time.

Chapter Thirteen

PROBLEM SOLVING AND RECOVERY

SNAPSHOTS OF ORGANIZATIONS AND PEOPLE WHO SOLVE PROBLEMS AND RECOVER WELL

Problem solving means thinking—and acting—ahead on behalf of a customer who's facing a challenge that no one could have predicted. Recovering requires resolving a shortcoming that results from someone making an error or dropping the ball. Both situations present you with stressed-out and unhappy customers. Even though situations that require this kind of intervention may start out as a Moments of Misery, they can become excellent opportunities to create Moments of Magic—as the following stories show.

Extra Credit

While traveling in Europe, my friend Bill lost his wallet, in which he had carried two credit cards. He immediately called both credit card companies to cancel his cards. Although both companies took care of him, one was significantly better at solving his dilemma.

The first credit card company canceled the card immediately and told Bill that a new card would be waiting for him when he arrived at the next hotel on his itinerary. He wasn't scheduled to arrive there, however, until three days from the time he called to report the lost cards. That solution was acceptable for Bill, but he still wished he'd been able to get his card sooner. He figured that he'd get someone from home to wire him enough money to cover the next three days of travel.

Then he called the second credit card company, which happened to be American Express.

American Express also took care of canceling Bill's card, but instead of making him wait three days to get a new card, they gave him the address of the local American Express office. There, a card would be waiting for him within two hours, and the office was just a brief cab ride away.

Now Bill has a story to tell. He's become an enthusiastic advocate—an evangelist—for American Express. Why? Because he knows how much more difficult those three days would have been if American Express hadn't solved his problem. It wasn't American Express's fault that he lost his wallet, but they sure took the opportunity to show how responsive they could be to a customer in need.

LESSON: There are two types of problems that we can solve for our customers: complaints and needs. Needs are the problems that aren't our fault but are opportunities for us to prove to customers why they should *always* do business with us.

Listening to the Fans

Upon taking over the St. Louis Blues hockey franchise, new owner Dave Checketts decided to raise ticket prices. It proved to be an unpopular move.

Of course, sports fans never *welcome* price hikes on tickets for the home team's games. However, this particular increase attracted more grumbling than most, for a couple of reasons. First, the whole league had recently struggled through a prolonged player strike that had tested the patience of fans everywhere. Second, after that strike had finally been resolved, the St. Louis Blues had managed to post one of the worst losing records in the history of professional sports. If the fans were mad at the Blues after the strike and the lousy performance on the ice that followed it, they were downright *furious* when Checketts boosted ticket prices. They stayed away in droves, and the Blues went from having some of the most loyal fans in the National Hockey League to having one of the worst attendance records in the league.

At that point, Checketts did something that a lot of sports executives don't do: He listened to the fans. He did extensive interviewing and polling and asked the fans what he could do to get them to come back. Three particular answers came back most often: First and foremost, they wanted to see a competitive team on the ice. They didn't necessarily expect to win a championship, but they wanted to see a team that won more often than it was at the moment. Second, they wanted a team with a better work ethic than the one they were witnessing lose games night after night. Fans weren't convinced that the team members actually *wanted* to win or that they were willing to put in the effort to do so. And finally, the fans told Checketts that they'd appreciate a break on the ticket prices he'd hiked up.

Dave Checketts let it be known that he, too, wanted the Blues to win and try hard, but that was out of his hands. He'd delegated that job to the coach. What he did have control over, though, was ticket prices. He reduced the prices and sent letters to fans telling them that he was committed to earning back their business. The fans started coming back!

Checketts stepped up and took ownership, not just of the team but also the problem. And he gave his fans a solution that worked.

LESSON ONE: If there's a big problem, talk to your customers and try to figure out exactly what it is.

LESSON TWO: Get to work. Set up a plan to solve the problem—then execute the plan.

LESSON THREE: Communicate with your customers. Tell them what you're doing to solve the problem.

The Pizza Reward

Sometimes you can solve a problem in a way that puts the accent on fun and lets everyone enjoy the process. Case in point: My father-in-law used to own a chain of retail pet stores. He would throw a pizza party for any of the stores that had an accident-free quarter. The employees loved the parties, and my father-in-law didn't have to pay workers' comp claims, which kept his insurance premiums down and (most important) kept employees safe! This is a great example of internal problem solving that promotes a positive work environment—one that put employees in a positive frame of mind and showed them that the company was invested in their well-being. And it was, from the company's point of view, a budgetary winner: $25 worth of pizza went a long way in boosting morale and saving money.

LESSON ONE: Giving employees an incentive (and one that doesn't cost the company a lot of money) can help solve internal problems.

LESSON TWO: Team celebrations are an excellent way to reward that incentive.

Why I Kept the Chicken

Not long ago, I had lunch with a buddy at one of my favorite Asian restaurants. One of their lunch specials was salmon with teriyaki sauce. We both felt like ordering it, so we asked the server, "Is the salmon teriyaki good?"

She jokingly said, "It's great. It tastes like chicken!" And we all laughed.

A few minutes later, out comes lunch. It did taste like chicken, because it *was* chicken! We'd both gotten the wrong order. (I think she might have written "chicken" on her order pad by mistake after our little joke.)

Our waitress came over to see how everything was at our table. When we told her the salmon really did taste like chicken and pointed to our dishes, she looked at our half-eaten meals and literally turned red with embarrassment. She said she was very, very sorry and told us that she wanted to get us the salmon as quickly as she could. We had a good laugh about the mistake and told her not to worry about it. We were fine with the chicken. That's what we had for lunch.

Why did we accept the wrong order? First and foremost, she'd had a good attitude about taking care of us throughout the exchange. If she'd tried to say that it wasn't her fault, or tried to argue that we'd somehow ordered chicken when we knew we hadn't, we might have had problems. Second, the chicken actually was pretty good! It wasn't what we ordered, but it was still tasty. Had we not liked it, we would have asked her to replace it as quickly as possible. Ultimately, though, it was her positive attitude that overcame the mistake. From the moment she came to the table, she was friendly, fun, engaging, and helpful.

LESSON: Sometimes customers will overlook problems if they know how much you care *and* if you have a great attitude throughout the process.

Fixing the People Problem First

A while back, I had a problem with my computer monitor. It was creating all kinds of interesting colors intermittently, and as cool as all those colors looked, I couldn't read what was on the screen. I called the manufacturer, and after I'd spent an hour waiting on the help line, the monitor stopped doing its little act—just a minute before I began talking to the person who was supposed to be able to help me. The person told me to call back when the screen was acting up again. I was frustrated, to say the least. Well, the monitor started doing its thing again, so I quickly called and somehow got right through to someone who was very helpful. He took a very different approach from the first service rep. He explained that the company would send a new monitor, which I could expect to receive within two business days.

What a difference between the first call and the second! And what made the difference possible? The answer is simple, and it has two parts.

The first and most noticeable distinction between the two employees was in their training. I'm assuming that the second person had simply received better product training, immediately recognized what my problem was, and was quicker to conclude that I simply had a broken monitor that was not worth trying to fix. The first person made me go through all kinds of tests to determine what the problem was. Since it wasn't acting up while we were talking, he assumed that there was nothing wrong with the monitor.

The second part of the answer is attitude, which is what *really* made the recovery possible. The second person realized that he was talking to a customer—not a piece of equipment. The first person, on the other hand, didn't seem very interested in helping us, because he was in troubleshooting mode and not in people mode. In the apparent absence of a technical problem, he had nothing to talk about.

There are two types of customer service reps out there: those who try to take care of the problem and those who take care of the customer.

LESSON: Take care of the customer first, and show the right attitude in doing so. Don't lose sight of the people problem in an effort to fix the technical problem.

Beyond "We're Out of That"

On a recent plane trip, I saw a flight attendant use her own creativity to take care of a simple passenger request. During the beverage service portion of the flight, someone who was seated near me asked for some iced tea. Sometimes there are cans of iced tea available; this time, however, there weren't. The flight attendant responded to the passenger's request by saying, "Usually we have cans of tea, but for some reason we don't today. Isn't iced tea just hot tea poured over ice? If you can wait a few minutes, I'll be happy to brew some hot tea and bring a cup of ice to go with it." She reappeared in a few minutes with a cup of freshly brewed tea, and the passenger was delighted.

Along the same lines, consider the Xerox customer who called the help line to report an error on his copier, expecting to have to schedule, and pay for, a service call because his warranty had expired. The Xerox representative could have spent a lot of time talking about whether the warranty had expired, but she chose not to do that, and as a result, she created a loyal customer in Xerox. The customer listened in astonishment as the Xerox representative identified the problem, tracked down the right part, and arranged for it to be shipped, free of charge, even though the copier was no longer under warranty! Because this was a part that the customer could easily install on his own, the Xerox rep used a little creativity, made a good business decision, showed some flexibility, and won an evangelist.

LESSON: Telling a customer you are out of something or can't take action is disappointing for everyone. Sometimes a little creativity and flexibility can not only solve the problem but also create a Moment of Magic!

The Auto Service Manager Who Got It

A friend of mine named Bob took his car to be serviced at one of the better-known national auto service chain centers. The service and repairs that his car required came to just over $100. Several days later, Bob drove out of town on a family vacation. Somewhere along the way, the car broke down, and the problem turned out to be exactly the one that had (supposedly) just been fixed. The service center's guarantee stated that Bob would have to bring the car back to their center or to another store in the chain if he wanted it to be fixed. However, Bob was 200 miles from the nearest store in the chain. Reluctantly, he paid for the repair at another shop.

When Bob returned from vacation, he stopped by the repair center and told the manager that he had had to pay for the same repair a second time. Despite the fact that the letter of the law in the repair center's guarantee said that the shop was not obligated to refund the money, the manager apologized and credited the money that Bob paid to his next service at the auto center. Bob had expected a fight, but he was instead pleasantly surprised by the manager's response to the problem. Clearly, this manager got it.

Notice three things that the manager did: First—and perhaps most notably—he took personal responsibility for the situation. Second, he looked past the letter of the law in the guarantee. After all, he knew that Bob had been doing business with his store for years. The $100 at stake was a small percentage of all of the business Bob was worth to his shop in years to come. Third, the manager issued, not a refund, but a *credit* for future service. The only way that Bob could get his money back was to return!

The manager didn't argue or question Bob (which is what made this great recovery moment possible). He simply took care of him. The credit toward future service was a reasonable way of giving both sides what they wanted. Bob eventually got his money back, and the manager kept him as a customer. That's a classic— but all too rare—win-win outcome!

LESSON ONE: Sometimes company policies are too focused on the company and not focused enough on the customer. Look beyond company policy to do what is right by the customer— especially when it makes complete sense to do so.

LESSON TWO: If you have to give something away, then give it away the next time the customer does business with you. This tells customers that you want them back and gives you a second chance to show how attentive you can be to their needs.

The Jacket Recovery

A while back, I was at a black-tie wedding at a luxury hotel. I watched in horror as a server spilled a tureen of hot au jus all over the jacket of a man sitting at the table next to mine. Instantly, the server asked the guest whether he was okay; he was. The server then asked the gentleman to take off his jacket so that the hotel could have it cleaned. The server promised to have the garment returned within 30 minutes. The table was in awe when the server returned 20 minutes later with the guest's clean jacket. It turned out that the hotel had a dry-cleaning facility on the premises, so it was actually not that complicated for the server to take immediate action to fix the problem. Even if the hotel didn't have the cleaning facility, they have a stellar reputation, and I'm sure that the waiter would have found a reasonable solution to the problem. (Of course, if he had been unable to clean the jacket in 30 minutes, he should never have offered a commitment to do so.)

It was obvious that the hotel had trained this employee not just in delivering great service but in the art of recovery. He saw the problem, realized what had to happen next, and did what was necessary to resolve the situation to the customer's satisfaction.

You may be interested to learn that the guest who got the au jus bath is now a repeat customer at this hotel! Further proof that great service—and great recovery—translates into repeat business.

LESSON: When there's a problem, take immediate action to solve it. Attempt to wow the customer with the recovery. Make a promise you can keep. Then, follow through on that promise.

Transportation Agitation

I stayed at a beautiful resort hotel not long ago that provided a nice service to its guests. It arranged for and scheduled (guest-paid) shuttle vans to the airport. This was convenient and far less expensive than taking a cab, and I was looking forward to taking advantage of the service. I guess I messed up their system, though, by checking out of my room a little too early. When I asked the young woman at the front desk to set up a van for me, she told me she couldn't find my name on the guest list. I told her that this was because I had checked out of the hotel that morning. My status as a former guest presented a problem, because the only way she had been trained in how to charge me for the van was to apply the fee to my room bill! She literally didn't know how to set up the transaction now that I was a former guest as opposed to a current guest.

This could have been a Moment of Misery; however, the resort knew that problems and complaints are opportunities to recover and deliver Moments of Magic. I reached out to the hotel manager and explained our problem to him. Wasn't there a way to get me on a van?

It turned out that the hotel had a policy against giving this special discounted ride to people who hadn't stayed at the hotel, and that certainly made economic sense from the hotel's point of view. Yet it didn't make sense to me. I had, after all, just stayed at the hotel! The manager figured out a way around the procedure of charging the room by accepting my payment as a so-called miscellaneous charge. He explained to the young woman at the front desk that she could feel free to follow this new procedure if the situation ever arose again.

The manager was customer-focused, the clerk was operations-focused, and the policy changed before my eyes. While I stood and watched them discuss the situation, he did something magical, something that told me exactly what kind of hotel I was staying at. Without ever coming across as overbearing or authoritarian, he showed her exactly how to move from an operations focus to a customer focus and reminded her which focus was driving the organization. I took the van to the airport, and I also witnessed a textbook example of a great recovery.

LESSON: Train employees on the importance of customer-focused thinking, and realize that you are teaching and encouraging people to identify the situations where it makes good business sense to be flexible with the rules and do right thing for both the company and the customer. By the way, it's perfectly acceptable to train, not reprimand, an employee to take a customer focus, rather than an operations focus, in front of the customer. Done the right way, it sends precisely the right message—to both the customer and the employee!

Trust Your Customers

There's a wonderful independent movie theater chain in St. Louis owned by a great guy named Harman Moseley. One night, my wife and I were in line to see a film at one of his theaters. We'd already bought our tickets and were moving forward into the theater. My wife stepped away from the long line for a moment to use the restroom. When she came back, she realized she'd left her ticket next to the sink when she washed her hands. Of course, when she went back to get the ticket, she couldn't find it. By the time she returned, she was feeling stressed because we were almost to the front of the line, and we were short one ticket.

Fortunately, there wasn't a problem. As luck would have it, Harman Moseley himself was standing there taking customers' tickets. When we explained our predicament to him, he smiled and said, "We trust our customers!" And he waved us through.

LESSON: Most customers are honest. All too often, rules and regulations are written with dishonest customers in mind. Consider rules that favor honesty. Look for ways to give your customers the benefit of the doubt.

Wheels of *Amazement*

Problems happen; that much is inevitable. The question is how you and your company will resolve those problems in a way that shows your customer that you're totally committed to delivering a positive outcome.

One of my favorite examples of a group that was able to solve a potentially disastrous problem—and keep its customer moving on the journey to the *cult of amazement*—is XTRA Lease, a trailer-leasing company based in St. Louis that I am proud to call a client. The company had a major problem on a big fleet of trailers they had leased to a customer. It seems that a manufacturing defect in some of the trailers' wheels caused a potentially unsafe condition. The lug nuts on these wheels were in danger of loosening, which meant the wheels could fall off the trailer while it was being pulled down the highway—a potentially *very* dangerous situation.

My client immediately took the customers' entire fleet of trailers off the road and contacted the manufacturer to look into the problem. The manufacturer determined that only 10 percent of the customer's fleet of trailers had been affected, and it committed to replacing only those 10 percent of the wheels that it knew to be unsafe. On the other hand, XTRA knew that its job was not only to fix the technical problem but also to restore the confidence of a customer. They paid to replace *all* of the wheels on the *entire* fleet, even though only a small portion had the defective wheels, and even though the problem was the manufacturer's fault. In the short term, this solution may have seemed expensive, but in the long run, the customer's confidence in XTRA more than repaid the investment.

LESSON: When your company faces an unfortunate situation, the goal is not only to fix the problem at hand but also to restore confidence. Doing the right thing may cost a little more than expected, but this may be what it takes to create customer loyalty.

Relieving the Headache

Way back in 1983, Johnson & Johnson's Tylenol pain reliever made headlines for all the wrong reasons. Someone had surreptitiously opened packages of Tylenol and inserted cyanide into the capsules. Johnson & Johnson's executive team faced a difficult decision: Should they recall every single package of Tylenol from every store in the United States, even though the tampering problem affected only a tiny fraction of the product currently in distribution?

The company's answer was a definitive Yes. Although the decision seemed prohibitively expensive to some, it proved to be *exactly* the right call. Johnson & Johnson knew that people were never going to buy an over-the-counter pain reliever unless they could trust the assurances of the manufacturer that the product was absolutely safe. The nationwide recall proved that the company was willing to act decisively and boldly on behalf of its customers. It was one of the many good decisions that Johnson & Johnson made to protect their consumers' faith in its brand. Tamper-evident packaging and a redesign of the capsule itself solidified Tylenol's position in the marketplace. It remains a leading product in the category today, despite the fact that many had predicted the brand would die as a result of the scare.

LESSON: When your product or service has a problem—especially one that's related to the safety and well-being of your customers—act boldly and without hesitation to take full responsibility for that problem and restore customer confidence.

Give Your People the Chance to Solve the Problem!

Nordstrom department stores have become legends in customer service. The first rule in the policy manual of the legendary apparel retailer reads as follows: *Use your own best judgment at all times.* The second rule reads as follows: *There will be no additional rules.*

Many organizations handcuff their team members when it comes to resolving customer problems. The now-famous Nordstrom's manual demonstrates a different approach. Everyone who works there gets the message that they are not only *allowed* to think independently when it comes to resolving the problems of customers but also *required* to do so as a matter of policy. A famous story about Nordstrom's commitment to keeping the customer satisfied tells how a man went to his local Nordstrom and returned a tire he said he had purchased there, receiving a full refund. *Nordstrom does not sell tires and never has,* but the previous proprietors, from whom Nordstrom's bought the location, *did* sell tires. According to this now-legendary account, a Nordstrom employee implemented Rule 1, and kept the customer happy, by issuing a refund on a product the company didn't even sell!

LESSON: Keep things simple for employees. Let them use their best judgment at all times when it comes to solving problems for customers.

The Connection That Almost Wasn't

I don't like to kick any industry when it's down, and the airline industry is—as I write these very words—encountering quite a bit of turbulence in the marketplace. So when I have the chance to say something nice about airline service, I like to take that opportunity.

Several years ago, I was fortunate enough to deliver a speech to the employees of Skywest Airlines, a regional commuter airline based in St. George, Utah. My topic was Moments of Magic, and after I was done speaking, the chairman of the board took the opportunity to share with the assembled team a letter from a passenger expressing gratitude to a Skywest agent for help in overcoming some potentially serious travel setbacks.

This passenger began his journey in San Francisco and was supposed to get a connecting flight in Los Angeles that would take him to Asia. Unfortunately, some weather problems caused the flight to Los Angeles to be delayed. Obviously, the man wanted to find a way to get to his connecting flight on time.

The agent first called a competing airline to see whether the passenger could get on that flight to L.A. The answer was yes, and the passenger thanked the agent for his help and sprinted over to the gate where his new flight was supposed to depart. No sooner did he show up there, though, than he got more bad news: This flight, too, was delayed. He turned around and ran back to the Skywest gate, which was now cleared to take off for L.A. It would be tight, but if there were no further delays, the passenger would have a small window of just a few minutes to make his flight to the Far East.

If the Skywest agent had done nothing more, he would have merited a fan letter. But he knew that the connection between the incoming flight from San Francisco and the outgoing flight to Asia still had one significant problem: Los Angeles International Airport. This agent knew the layout of the airport and was concerned that the distance between the two gates was too great, since they were on opposite sides of the airport. He called ahead and told the Skywest team in Los Angeles about the tight connection. They met the customer at the arrival gate and drove him to his departure gate in an electric cart—and he made the connection!

How long do you think this passenger is going to remember how well he was treated?

LESSON: Sometimes recovery happens *before* an anticipated problem takes place. This requires thinking ahead. In this case, a phone call to a *competitor*, and then to a competent fellow employee, solved a customer's problem. Look for ways to think ahead on behalf of your customer!

Long-Distance Recovery

My long-distance carrier nearly lost me a few years back when I learned from a competitor about a similar program that was substantially less expensive than what I was used to paying. The savings was upwards of 20 percent. When I learned of the money-saving plan that the competitor was offering me, I immediately called my current long-distance carrier to ask why they didn't offer such a plan. I was curious to learn what they might offer me as an incentive to stay with them. I was surprised and upset to learn that for the last two years they had offered an identical plan!

I asked why the carrier hadn't informed me of this plan, and the customer service representative told me that a promotional piece was probably mailed to me at some point. That didn't make me feel any better. It seemed there should have been some kind of system that would have automatically switched me over to the better plan. What customer, after all, would object to a plan that cost less?

The customer service person could sense my frustration and offered to give me a 15 percent credit on every bill I had paid over the past two years, on the condition that I agree to stay with the company as my long-distance carrier. Notice that she built the refund around my hot button issue—the two years I had been overpaying—and that she found a way to connect the refund to a commitment to stay on as a customer. It was a pretty good deal that amounted to a couple of months of free long-distance service for me, and of course, they immediately switched me to the best plan they had at that time. I stuck with the company.

LESSON ONE: When structuring a refund or credit, try to connect it to the customer's hot button issue. This isn't about making a concession just to make a customer happy; it's about positioning the refund or credit as a direct response to the problem or complaint.

LESSON TWO: If you are in a refund situation, try to apply it to future business. This may get the customer back in the door and give you the opportunity to do it right the next time.

The Bottom Line

Some of your customers may be facing unexpected problems that are not your organization's fault. They can cause stress and anxiety. Use these situations as opportunities to demonstrate your willingness to take creative action on the customer's behalf.

Other customers may be experiencing Moments of Misery that are your fault. Remember that you *want* customers to complain when they are unhappy, because once you know they are unhappy, you can take action to turn the Moment of Misery into a Moment of Magic! *A complaining customer can be your best opportunity to show how good you are . . . and to create a customer evangelist!*

Chapter Fourteen

OPPORTUNITY KNOCKS

ORGANIZATIONS AND PEOPLE WHO LOOK FOR OPPORTUNITIES TO BE BETTER THAN AVERAGE

W ow! They didn't have to do that.'' But they did—and you remembered the experience. Consider the following true stories of organizations that identified and took advantage of opportunities to set themselves apart from the competition.

Managing the Experience

I bought a hamburger at an airport fast-food restaurant on a recent trip. The total bill came to $6.07. The young man at the counter—his name was Matt—noticed me fumbling for change and asked, "Do you have the seven cents?"

I told him that I didn't. Before I could pull out another dollar bill, the young man took my six dollars and told me not to worry about the seven cents. He took seven pennies from the share-a-penny tray that was next to the register, smiled, and said, "Now you won't be jingling around all day."

It was a small but considerate gesture—and such a nice line—that I mentioned the positive exchange to the restaurant manager a few minutes later. That's when I discovered that what I experienced with Matt was more the norm than the exception. The manager had coached his entire team to shave off a few cents when it looked like doing so could be a convenience to the customer. This manager knew full well that there was more than one job to do. First was the job of taking the customer's order, and then there was the job of taking care of the customer! He had plenty of other taking-care-of-the-customer moments, along with other snappy, upbeat lines, that he had trained his team to perform. What a great example of managing the customer experience!

LESSON: Train your team to expect and take advantage of the most common opportunities they will encounter in order to deliver an above-average customer experience.

Do What It Takes

Years ago, I was having some challenges getting the mortgage for my first home, not because I couldn't afford the loan payments but because I was young and self-employed. The bankers I talked to treated me like I was applying for a *business* loan. They spent all their time looking over my cash flow figures and my business plan. I was an opportunity waiting to be discovered for a banker who was willing to look at me as a person—not as a bunch of numbers on loan application documents.

Then along came Hord Hardin, a banker I knew from attending school with his son. I ran into Mr. Hardin at a charity fund-raiser. I explained my situation to him, and he agreed to meet with me to discuss a home loan. I ended up sitting down with Hord, going over my last two years of tax returns, showing off my upcoming (almost full) speaking calendar, and filling out a few simple forms. The entire process took less than half an hour. Surprisingly, Hord and his bank approved my loan on the spot. Even more important, Hord and I had connected as people.

LESSON: Treat your customers like people, not like numbered accounts. When we open ourselves up to having real relationships with *people*, we find ways to make the right things happen.

The Luxury Loaner

I bought my last car from Plaza Motors, a St. Louis dealership that carries a variety of makes of cars. My sales rep at the time was Harl White. Harl was always looking for, and finding, opportunities to improve my relationship with the dealership. Once I had my car in for service, and Harl arranged for me to use a loaner while the repairs were being done. Unfortunately, the loaner was a compact car. Normally this wouldn't have been a problem; however, I was picking up three clients at the airport the next morning. I wanted to create a good impression, and cramming them into a car with virtually no back seat wasn't going to do it.

I explained my situation to Harl, who arranged on the spot for me to drive away in a luxury loaner at no extra charge. This brand new, very large car would give my clients the comfortable ride they deserved—and make a great impression. And telling them about how Harl took care of *them*—and not just me—would make for a great story.

Harl listened to my problem and didn't waste a moment. He gave me exactly what I needed.

LESSON: By taking care of his own client—me—Harl allowed me to take care of my own clients. Keep a lookout for ways to dramatically upgrade the experience of a favored customer. The results may affect more people than you'd ever expect.

Used, New—We Don't Care. We Made It!

I try to keep tabs on great customer service stories that pop up in newspapers and magazines and on the Internet. The following account demonstrated a truly great commitment to servicing the product, no matter what the situation.

No doubt you've seen the Segway, the electric-powered, two-wheeled transportation unit that people use to zoom around airports, warehouses, and other places that used to be the exclusive domain of pedestrians. The online forum SegwayChat (http://forums.segwaychat.com/) featured a post from an owner who had bought a *used* Segway. Buying from a third party meant that he had no contact whatsoever with the manufacturer, only with the person who sold him the unit. Although his Segway worked well, he wanted to customize the look a little bit, so he picked up an optional set of splash guards on eBay. The problem was that the online retailer who from whom he had purchased the splash guards had sent him the wrong size washers. He called the local Segway dealer to see if he could buy a new set of washers.

Without hesitation, the Segway dealer sent him a full set of washers and screws for free—via Federal Express! He had them the next day. In return, the happy customer rushed to the Internet to share his great customer service story with the rest of the world. Although Segway had played no part in the initial transaction, they were quick to save the day and respond to a Segway owner.

LESSON: Don't get distracted by whether a prospective long-term customer bought your product from you or someone else.

Make the customer's initial experience with you easy and memorable. Do it right, and you'll earn an evangelist for life.

The Cake That Didn't Melt

I was pleasantly surprised to learn that Thrifty Foods, a British Columbia–based retailer, has a policy of supplying a free birthday cake to any and every family with a child who's turning one year old. You read that right: They give a *free cake* to any family that stops by one of their locations and places the order for an upcoming first birthday. (And by the way, it is not a tiny promotional cake. It's a full-sized cake that can feed 10 or more people.)

This policy alone would have entitled Thrifty to a place of honor in this book, but what the company did for one family takes their service to a whole new level. I'll quote from a letter the father wrote to the company.

> To whom it may concern,
>
> I want to tell you about the fantastic experience we had with the Thrifty Foods in Coquitlam, Austin Station, this past weekend.
>
> Our son was turning one year-old. My wife ordered a cake through the bakery as part of your first birthday promotion. We picked the cake up on Friday afternoon; it was nicely decorated with his name. However, by the time we got home, the afternoon heat had caused the icing to slide and melt off the sides of the cake. My wife was nearly in tears; we had family coming to stay, and nearly 40 people arriving the next afternoon to celebrate Nicholas' birthday.
>
> I called the customer service line and explained what happened. I was referred to the store, where I retold my story twice more. Everyone was super understanding. Finally,
>
> (*continued*)

(continued)

I spoke to "Ray," whom I assume was the duty manager. He had obviously been briefed by someone else, because he apologized for not having a cake decorator in the store at that moment. He promised to communicate our situation to Trent, the bakery manager. He arranged for me to take the cake back to Trent and have him look at it to see what he could do. I was very relieved. I didn't want to spend the night trying to recreate the icing on the cake.

The next day, I took the cake to the bakery department. I was greeted by one of the staff who already knew about our situation. She got Trent, who took the cake and told me to return in 15 minutes. When I came back he presented me with what I suspect was a new cake—although I don't know for sure.

Disaster Averted!!!!

I was stunned by the helpfulness and understanding of everyone I spoke to; especially since this was a free cake to begin with.

There isn't just one person who deserves credit for this; it's the whole team, from the Customer Service person on the toll free line, to the evening staff at the store and Trent the Bakery Manager.[1]

I'd like you to notice a couple of things about this story. First and foremost, *none of the problems with the cake was Thrifty's fault.* The company had done absolutely nothing wrong. Second, the family *had not bought anything!* The cake was free, and the company would have been perfectly within its rights to point out that free cakes come with no warranty.

Clearly, the Thrifty employees were after something very different than proving whether they were right or whether they had done anything wrong. It saw an opportunity to avert disaster on behalf of a (potential!) customer. In averting that disaster, they earned themselves an evangelist—and, I suspect, a lifetime customer.

LESSON: Even when you have done nothing wrong, you can still help a customer avert a disaster. Seize these opportunities to show how good you can be.

The Santa Claus Paradox

Do you remember Edmund Gwenn as Santa Claus in the classic film *Miracle on 34th Street?* (Gwenn won an Oscar for best supporting actor for his performance.) When a customer asked Gwenn, playing Kris Kringle, a Macy's department store Santa—for help in finding a certain product, he smiled and referred the person to a competitor: Gimbels!

There's a paradox at work here, one that *New York Times* tech writer David Pogue confirms in an August 5, 2006, post on the *Times* technology blog. Pogue asked the local Toyota dealership for help in replacing the six-year-old (and, apparently, irreparable) audio system in his Toyota minivan. The gist of the service rep's response: We could put a new one in for you, but you'll pay less and get more features with a nonfactory model.

The incident stuck with Pogue, and it instantly reminded me of the Santa Claus story. When a company's people are up front with us about the best options we face, we tend to remember the experience and remain loyal to the organization. Call it the Santa Claus paradox! This reminds me of a restaurant that my wife and I visited. It had been open only a few weeks. We had a great dinner, after which we had a long and pleasant conversation with the owner. Rather than trying to sell us on coming back soon, he spent much of his time with us recommending other restaurants in the area for us to visit!

This took us a bit by surprise. I think the owner's confidence in the dining experience he had just delivered to us was part of what made it feel so natural for him to share those restaurant recommendations. He wasn't telling us that the restaurants he was recommending were *better* than his. He was saying, "I know you'll be back soon enough. In the meantime, let's talk about other places you'd like."

LESSON ONE: Know you're so good at what you do that you have the confidence to praise your competitors.

LESSON TWO: When you know for sure that the customer will benefit by going somewhere else, say so. You'll build trust and loyalty in the relationship.

Give and You Shall Receive

A new client had booked me for a speech. As a gesture of appreciation, I sent their top five executives complementary copies of my books. The cost of these books was small, and I didn't really think of the exercise as an investment in anything, other than a good relationship with a new client. This was simply a gesture of goodwill.

You can imagine how nice it felt to learn that the client was impressed enough by my gesture to order 200 copies of each book.

This experience led me to develop a new selling rule that I now make a point of executing whenever we book a speech with a new client. You may have heard the line from the movie *Field of Dreams* that says, "If you build it, they will come." My sales spin on it is "Give it away, and they will buy!"

LESSON: Ultimately, great service is about taking care of the customer by providing higher-than-average levels of service. Sometimes great service turns out to be your best sales force.

The Bottom Line

Don't just wait for your customers to come up with suggestions of how you can deliver an above-average customer experience. Examine your touch points (discussed in Chapter 11) to find opportunities to raise the bar and distinguish you and your organization from the competition!

Chapter Fifteen

PROACTIVE SERVICE AND FOLLOW-THROUGH

SNAPSHOTS OF PROACTIVE ORGANIZATIONS AND PEOPLE IN ACTION

Sometimes, a businessperson's willingness to take the initiative on behalf of the customer seems to be a lost art. Consider the following true stories, each from a company that has redis-covered and mastered that art and made it part of "how we do business here" with both internal and external customers.

Step Out!

Not long ago, I was staying at one of the Disney hotels in Orlando and found myself in a long line at the check-in counter. There were at least eight employees behind the front desk, so I was moving along at a pretty good speed. When I got to the front of the line, I saw that the open attendant was at the end of the front desk farthest from where I was standing. Before I could move, she walked out, greeted me, and asked me to come over to her area to check in. In other words, she walked me over to her desk! And *all* of the front desk personnel did the same thing when their area opened up for the next guest.

Compare that with what had happened at the (very expensive) hotel at which I had stayed the night before in New York City. When it was my turn to check in, the guy at the front desk yelled, "Next!" When I walked up to him, he didn't welcome me. He just said, "Name?" And that was it. The Disney employee took the initiative to *physically* come out to greet me, and she made sure that I felt welcomed as I arrived at the hotel. I walked the same distance I would have if she'd simply shouted, "Next!" The simple act of coming to escort me was what made this encounter memorable. And you can bet that I had—and told people about—a *very* different experience than I had at my hotel in New York.

LESSON: Stand out—and step out. Find a way—literally and figuratively—to meet your customer more than halfway.

Our First Priority: Employees

"Treat your employees the way you want your customers treated—maybe even better!" You may remember this quote from earlier chapters. When I first shared this principle in my online newsletter *The Shepard Letter,* I received the following case study by a freelance writer from Ohio named Andrew Thomas, about the legendary Ritz-Carlton Hotel chain.

Andrew wrote: "The Ritz-Carlton was hired to manage an existing hotel in Shanghai. They brought in many of their experts and determined that major renovations were needed; and the first phase of this overhaul was the employee entrance! This may seem strange to most; but it is the norm for the Ritz-Carlton. While this particular renovation was relatively inexpensive, it sent an important message to the employees, who had, up to that point, been employed by another hotel management company.

The choice to make the employee entrance the top priority demonstrated that a new, higher, standard of quality and service was now expected; and it clearly showed that the employees were an incredibly important part of the process.''

At a critical moment, the management at the Ritz-Carlton took the initiative to send the right message to their (new) employees. Some other hotel companies might have simply sent a memo in this situation: "We expect you to treat the guests well!" Ritz-Carlton took a much more effective approach. Management *modeled* the behavior it wanted to see, namely, treating the guests like VIPs. It had done so in an unforgettable way: *by treating the employees themselves like VIPs!*

A clear willingness to proactively invest in employees first is one of the main reasons the Ritz-Carlton is recognized worldwide as one of the premier hotel chains. Why? In large measure, it's because the management at Ritz-Carlton makes it absolutely clear that it is ready to treat its employees—its *internal* customers—like *ladies and gentlemen who will be serving ladies and gentlemen.*

LESSON ONE: Take the initiative to put employees first.

LESSON TWO: Model your own behavior toward employees on the way you want your customers treated.

The Pre-Event Touch

When we book a training program or speaking engagement at Shepard Presentations, we don't simply show up and deliver the program on the day of the event. In addition to all the initial logistical discussions around identifying the right days and times and locations, we have a system of pre-event touches in place.

A pre-event touch is all of the planned advance contact that we have with our clients. For example, once a training date is booked, one of our trainers contacts the client four weeks before the event to have a phone conversation about the content of the meeting. One week prior to the event, that same trainer calls, just to check in. Even though the main contact the client has is with our trainers, I always do a final check-in call to make sure that the client is confident and that everything is going according to plan. These calls are scheduled at specific times.

All of this pre-event contact sometimes takes people by surprise—especially the call from me. The clients certainly seem pleased to get a call from the owner of the company, which usually isn't what they expected, but that is just the way we do business. We manage the touch points during the entire process, but the *pre-event touches* create confidence for our clients—before our trainer even presents the program. The ultimate compliment comes when our new clients—who haven't yet gone through our program—recommend us to others. The reason, at least in part, is the confidence arising from the contact we make with them before we even provide our service.

LESSON ONE: Look for opportunities to connect voice to voice or face to face with your clients and customers *before* you deliver your service or product.

LESSON TWO: Remember that customers love to be contacted by the owner of the company or some other high-level executive.

Looking around the Corners

A while back, I had the opportunity to refinance my home mortgage and decided to work with an agent named Vicki Groswald. Vicki is one of those people who makes everything as easy as possible and who is particularly good at *looking around corners*. Before I could ask how long the application process would take, she told me it would take less than 15 minutes—and she was right. She advised me ahead of time exactly how much everything would cost, and she was right about that, too. She had the answers to my questions before I even knew what my questions were.

I was also impressed with the way that Vicki followed up after the sale. Once my new loan closed, she checked in with me—and the title company—to make sure everything had gone well. Even though her responsibility was technically finished once the loan was applied for and approved, she stayed along for the entire process. Vicki is at the top of my list for anticipating my questions and following through after the sale.

LESSON ONE: Anticipate the customer's questions. Give customers answers before they even have a chance to ask.

LESSON TWO: Be proactive with your follow-through. This gives you the opportunity to know everything has been taken care of and allows you to respond to any problems or complaints.

The List

Every December, just before the holidays, we do an exercise at my company where we make a list of all the people we've worked with over the past 10 years but somehow haven't talked to over the past 12 months. Once we compile the list, I use it to call each customer personally. I express my appreciation for past business, but I don't ever bring up the question of future business unless they do. It is merely a catching-up call. I like to ask my clients how they are doing, how their families are doing, and what's been going on in their lives. It's a chance to converse on a personal level. Of course, if they want to talk about business, they can, and they do. And even though I make it a rule to never bring up the topic of new business, these calls end up generating revenue for our company.

We also do this with the vendors who have helped us over the year. This is kind of a role reversal, since the vendors are usually thanking *us* for our business, but we like to let them know we appreciate them as well. When you take the initiative to connect first—even (especially!) when you don't have a formal reason—you show that you are personally interested in improving your relationships with both customers and vendors. And isn't that what the cult of the customer is all about?

LESSON: Make a list. (Check it twice.) Stay in touch. Show your appreciation.

A Tale of Two Waiters

In my opinion, the type of service that I receive at restaurants can be divided into two basic categories: proactive and everyone else.

Here's an example of proactive service: Without having to be summoned, the server notices that your water glass is nearly empty and silently glides over to refill it, without interrupting your conversation.

Here's an example of everyone else's kind of service: Your water glass is completely drained, and you can't seem to catch the eye of your server—or any server—for 10 minutes. That's what the principle might look like in the restaurant environment.

Of course, there are half-empty water glasses waiting to be filled in every industry. There are always problems you can take the initiative to solve *before* those problems cause customers to complain. One of my favorite examples comes from Southwest Airlines, which makes a point of *initiating* contact with customers who are inconvenienced by weather-related delays. In many cases, Southwest *offers* its weather-delayed passengers flight vouchers for a free flight—when the passengers haven't even asked for them or complained in any way. That's proactive service![1]

Which do you think is more likely to hasten your customer's journey to the *cult of amazement:* proactive service or everyone else service?

LESSON: Metaphorically speaking, what is the water glass in your business? Check the water in that glass before you're asked to.

Confirmation Turns into Confidence

It was the end of a long day on a recent business trip, and I was settling into my hotel bed. It was almost midnight, and I needed a cab to pick me up at the early hour of 4:30 A.M. for my flight home. I called the hotel operator to set up a wake-up call for 4:00 A.M. I also asked if there were usually cabs outside the hotel at that hour.

She asked, "What time would you like a cab?"

I told her, "I'd like a cab at half past four."

She said, confidently, that she would take care of it. I sure hoped she would. About five minutes later, the phone rang. I thought to myself, "Who could be calling me at this time of night? Someone must be calling the wrong room by mistake." Somewhat irritated, I answered the phone. To my surprise, it was the very same operator that I had just talked to moments before. She told me a cab would be waiting for me at 4:30 A.M. sharp. She also told me the name of the cab company, which impressed me, and the name of the driver who would be picking me up, which impressed me even more. I thanked her for setting all that up for me. She wished me a good night. Now I knew there wouldn't be a problem with getting the cab! I slept a lot better than I otherwise would have.

The next morning, the wake-up call came as scheduled. It was one of those recordings, thanking me for staying at the hotel and wishing me a good day. Within a minute or so, the phone rang again. This time it was the bellhop telling me my cab would be waiting for me at 4:30.

In my line of work, I often find myself waiting for a cab in the early hours of the morning. And there are many times when I find myself nervously waiting for a cab that was supposed to be there to take me to the airport. Not this time! I had complete confidence that I would be right on time for my flight home.

Winning—and deserving—your customers' confidence is part of delivering the consistently above-average experience that leads toward the *cult of amazement.*

LESSON: Confirm (and occasionally reconfirm) your customers' requests, and you will win their confidence.

E-Mail Me! Tell Me That Everything's Going According to Plan!

E-mail has its pros and cons. People complain about getting too much in one breath, but in the next, they express appreciation about how e-mail messages get them timely responses and quick information from customers, employees, and vendors.

When you order a book from Amazon.com, they send you an e-mail confirmation that your order has been received and then another one informing you when the order has been shipped. The same thing happens when you buy shoes from Zappos.com, a computer from Dell, and clothing from L.L. Bean. Many companies now take this step; some of them even send you the tracking number for the freight company (UPS, USPS, Federal Express, etc.) that's doing the shipping. This does more than just inform the customer. It delivers confidence!

LESSON: Confirmation e-mails are not only acceptable but also essential if you hope to instill confidence in your prospects and customers. Send them! E-mail is a powerful tool that helps you let your customer know, every step of the way, exactly what is happening with an order.

Starbucks's Three-Hour Coffee Break

When is a cup of coffee more than just a cup of coffee? When the promise to the customer depends on it. At one point, Starbucks closed down each and every one of its North American outlets—that's approximately 7,000 stores—for a three-hour period. Why? Because CEO Howard Schultz wanted to make sure that every employee took part in a special training session on how to make the perfect cup of Starbucks coffee. Schultz wanted his people to get back to basics. He wanted to be sure they understood that the foundation of their success was twofold: a great cup of coffee and outstanding customer service. Taking the initiative to schedule that special session on one day, versus over an extended period of time (perhaps months), let everyone know how important the organization's priorities were.

What did it cost Starbucks to close their stores to customers for those three hours? All of the employees were paid, and no customers were served. A bigger and better question: What would it have cost Starbucks *not* to proactively let employees know—in a dramatic, direct, and experiential way—about the organization's top priorities?

LESSON: Be proactive—and even a little dramatic—in letting everyone in your organization know about your organization's top priorities.

The Bottom Line

By anticipating concerns, needs, and problems ahead of time and by taking action early, you can show customers and employees alike exactly where you're headed: into the *cult of amazement.*

Chapter Sixteen

THE ART OF WOW

SNAPSHOTS OF TRULY *AMAZING* ORGANIZATIONS AND PEOPLE

Some experiences are so powerful that we can't help being *amazed*. Although you don't have to deliver at this level *all* the time, it sure helps build customer and employee loyalty if you try. In this chapter, you'll find astonishing examples of Hall of Fame service experiences.

It Didn't Absolutely, Positively *Have* to Be Here Overnight, but It Was!

I've already told you about Zappos.com, the online shoe and apparel retailer that takes pride in delivering WOW! moments to its customers. I had a particularly impressive encounter with them that proved the company's commitment to that standard. I placed an order with Zappos, and the e-mail I received shortly after placing the order was more than just a confirmation of my order. It shared a piece of very good, totally unexpected news.

Here's what the e-mail said:

Although you originally ordered Standard (4 to 5 business days) shipping and handling, we have given your order special priority processing in our warehouse and are upgrading the shipping and delivery time frame for your order. Your order will ship out today and be given a special priority shipping status so that you can receive your order even faster than we originally promised! Please note that this is being done at no additional cost to you. It is simply our way of saying thank you for being our customer.

WOW! I placed the order on a Wednesday, and it arrived on Thursday! Question one: Did you notice that Zappos told me *ahead of time* about the unexpected shipping upgrade? That e-mail gave me *two* Moments of Magic for the price of one: that moment when I read the e-mail and the moment when the merchandise arrived as promised!

Question two: Do you think I will buy again from Zappos? Of course!

Question three: How many people do you suppose I shared that story with? Dozens of people? Hundreds of people? Try hundreds of thousands of people! I quickly posted the unexpected e-mail from Zappos on the Internet! How could you *not* fall in love, and start evangelizing for, a company that places such a clear priority on WOWing its customers?

LESSON: When you find a way to dramatically exceed your customer's expectations, let them know it. Exploit it. Do it right, and you'll get two Moments of Magic for the price of one.

Break a Rule or Two

I've heard of on-the-spot refunds, but I don't think I've ever come across one quite like this. A customer in England ordered a bag from the trendy urban accessories company Timbuk2, only to find that a decorative Velcro patch on the bag was defective. The customer requested a refund and received this response via e-mail:

> Since I'm not all about weighing down a plane with broken product that we will simply look at and say "Yep, it's broken," and since I'm all about people passing on good intentions, this is what has happened, and what you need to do: I sent you a credit to replace the bag. No need to send it to us, your dodgy picture is proof enough (for me; this isn't exactly "by the book," so don't expect all the customer service people to do this, k?). Order yourself a new bag. But! Bring your Velcro-impaired bag to a place that takes donations, whether that place be Goodwill, a homeless dude down the street, or your broke best friend. Don't throw the bag away! Give it away to someone who needs a bag—regardless of that bag's Velcro status. No funny business, ya' hear?[1]

Great story! Great response! Great Moment of Magic!

Perhaps you're wondering: Was it the CEO of the company who made that decision? No. It was just someone who'd been *empowered* by the CEO to do the right thing for the customer. When the CEO of Timbuk2 saw the story on a public bulletin board, he posted this message for all to see:

> I am the CEO at Timbuk2 . . . and I wanted to say—thank you for the posting. I am very proud of the team here.
>
> 1. They made this call on their own.
> 2. They broke the rules that should be broken.
> 3. It all worked well.
>
> I also wanted to let you know that we are a small enough factory we are also looking into what happened to allow the quality to slip like that—so the factory team is figuring that out. Thank you.

LESSON ONE: Empower the team to make the best call they can.

LESSON TWO: Empower them to break the rules that should be broken.

Bring It In!

I almost couldn't believe this one, but it's legitimate. I read about a man who had purchased a Wii game console from Nintendo for his son but found, after two weeks, that there was a problem with the unit. It was vibrating for some reason, and it kept getting louder and louder as any game was being played. Clearly, it needed some kind of repair. Dad wasn't looking forward to telling his six-year-old that the household's favorite toy was about to go out of commission for a couple of weeks, but eventually he accepted the inevitable and called the Nintendo help line to try to arrange for repairs.

The call was going well; the customer service representative asked for the family's phone number. When she heard it, she asked, ''Are you here in the state of Washington?''

Dad answered that he was and mentioned that he lived in Redmond.

As it happens, Redmond, Washington, is the very town where Nintendo of America's campus was located. The customer service rep told him to skip the trouble and delay of packaging up the unit. He should simply bring the unit in to the Nintendo campus. That day, right away. The company would fix the unit while he and his son waited. She gave him directions to the campus.

Still half-convinced that someone, somewhere, was pulling his leg, the dad got in the car and drove to the campus, where he and his son were, just a few minutes later, greeted by costumed Nintendo characters. He explained his situation to the woman who was waiting for him at the reception area, and 30 minutes later, the Wii unit had been repaired.

LESSON: Fix problems as quickly as possible. If you can possibly find a way to do so, offer to fix the problem right away, while the customer waits.

Storm? What Storm?

I came across an article in the *Arizona Republic* newspaper (July 22, 2008) that told the story of a Phoenix man who found himself in a three-car collision but still managed to make it to the restaurant where he had a dinner reservation for the evening. What does that have to do with customer service? Everything! Shortly after he emerged (unhurt) from the hit-and-run collision, motorist Gerard Montemurro picked up his cell phone and called Marcellino Ristorante to explain what happened and inform the restaurant that he and his friend weren't going to be using their table that evening.

The owner of the restaurant offered to pick up Montemurro. Initially, Montemurro said no, but after waiting an unreasonable amount of time in the rain for a tow truck to retrieve their car and pick them up, he decided to call back and see if he could take up the good people at Marcellino Ristorante on their offer. Sima and Marcellino Veriza—the husband-and-wife team who own and operate the restaurant—agreed to swing by and pick up Montemurro and his friend near a freeway off-ramp.

They even brought dry clothes with them!

According to the *Arizona Republic,* Montemurro had high praise for his rescuers. "It was just pretty extraordinary. Not only from a customer-service standpoint, but just from a human-being standpoint," Montemurro said.

Once Montemurro and his friend had completed their multi-course Italian dinner, the Verizas drove them back to their vehicle so they could hook up with their tow truck driver!

LESSON: Sometimes our customer's problems aren't our fault. It may be that the customer is just having a bad day. Still, their problems can be our opportunities to show how great we are.

Problem Solved: Here's a New Computer!

Apple Computer has generated legions of evangelists as a result of its stellar service on the company's MacBook computers and other products. Here's a true story that proves how far the company is willing to go to keep its customers satisfied—and loyal—when they need maintenance on their Mac products.

A MacBook user sent his laptop computer in for some work. The Apple folks ended up fixing his problem by upgrading the customer to a new, more expensive, and more powerful MacBook—at no charge! He simply received a brand-new computer in the mail that had his old computer's data downloaded onto the hard drive. If the Apple people didn't have a customer for life before they came up with this creative workaround, I bet they do now.[2]

LESSON: Sometimes the best fix is not to fix but to replace—or even upgrade. When you do it with the right attitude, expeditiously and with no hassle, you create confidence, which eventually leads to loyalty.

Waiter, Please Check My Locker

Morton's Steakhouse is one of my clients—and one that, I am proud to say, offers a unique experience to its high-end diners, an experience that both wows them and encourages them to come back again and again. The restaurant provides their patrons with a personal wine locker, where they can store their favorite bottles of wine for later enjoyment with the restaurant's fine food. Customers can purchase bottles or cases of wine on-site and store unused bottles for later visits. The locker program has become quite popular with Morton's guests, because it allows them to guarantee availability of their favorite wines. It also supports a major interest of many of the restaurant's guests: learning more about which fine wines best complement a given dish. Once a good wine-and-entrée combination has been established, the locker system allows restaurant-goers to repeat the experience with associates, friends, and loved ones on a future visit to Morton's.

This is a great example of a *true* loyalty program, one that's based on giving customers an experience they want to repeat. Many so-called loyalty programs—for example, some (but not all) of the major airlines' frequent-flier loyalty programs—are little more than administrative mazes with hard-to-redeem rewards attached to them. These aren't really loyalty programs; they are, instead, attempts to make it inconvenient for the customer to switch to a competitor. Customers are loyal only because of the points, not because they enjoy the experience. If you're interested in making the journey to *amazement*, you'll build loyalty by offering the customer a positive experience that no one else is providing.

LESSON: Build customer loyalty around experiences that the customer actually wants to repeat and can only get from you.

No Problem—I'll Drop It Off on My Way Home

Shipping company DHL competes with Federal Express, UPS, and others in the fiercely competitive business of overnight package delivery. I recently heard a story about a DHL customer who was expecting a package, didn't receive it, and got a lesson in the art of WOW! from the recovery that DHL provided. Not only did DHL refund this particular customer's money for the ship-ment; they communicated the status of the package, apologized for the breakdown of the truck that had caused the delay, and then went above and beyond the call of duty to deliver the material to their customer.

The DHL driver whose truck had broken down ended up *driving his personal vehicle to the customer's home* to deliver the package that evening on his way home from work! As the customer reports, "To be honest, I thought he would be very upset that his boss made him come out on his way home and give me my package; but he seemed very happy to be able to do it. It felt like it might have even been his idea."[3]

In the end, what the customer remembered most was the DHL employee's *attitude* as he delivered the (late!) package. He was friendly, attentive, and most important, seemed *pleased* to be able take an action that extended far beyond the parameters of his regular duties. Notice how the emotional message that the employee sent helped DHL to transform a Moment of Misery into a Moment of Magic!

LESSON: Doing the right thing is what the customer expects. How do you make it even better? By using your own *positive attitude* toward customers who have received less than your best and by turning a Moment of Misery into a WOW! moment.

The CEO Would Like to Handle This for You

Getting a top executive to invest a few minutes in a customer is another substantial way to create an evangelist. A customer of Photojojo.com, an online digital photography supply retailer, was in a hurry to find a particular component for his digital camera. Unfortunately, the customer missed the deadline for overnight delivery from Photojojo. When he called the company to explain his dilemma, the representative did a little digging and realized that the customer and the founder of the company were, at that moment, in the same city. The founder happened to have one of the components with him. Since the customer was in the neighborhood, would he be willing to meet the founder in person and pick up the component?

He was—and he did.[4] It is seemingly unbelievable that a company's CEO would go out of his way to ensure that one of his customers received a piece of equipment; however, this is just the kind of extraordinary experience that turns customers into staunch supporters.

I was also bowled over by a recent news report pointing out that Peter Liu, the founder and cochairman of San Francisco's environmentally friendly New Resource Bank, takes the time to read each e-mail that his customers submit via the bank's web site and that every once in a while, Liu personally responds to customer queries. Understand that New Resource is not a small-time operation; this bank has over $180 million in assets! When Liu answered a customer's question about ATM fees, the recipient could hardly believe the return e-mail address—or the extended e-mail discussion that followed.[5]

LESSON: If you can do so, find a way to leverage contact with top executives in a way that improves the customer experience. You'll leave a trail of WOW! responses in your wake!

Home Sweet Auto Dealership

In my experience, getting an oil change or minor service on my car used to boil down to an hour or two of wasted time. Fortunately, Plaza Motors in St. Louis has taken a little of the sting out of getting a car serviced. Plaza is a major auto dealership that specializes in high-end brands such as Lexus, Mercedes, Range Rover, Cadillac, and Porsche. The cars are exquisite, of course, but Plaza's management knows that it is ultimately the quality of the *service* experience that keeps its customers coming back.

That's why Plaza invested $23 million to upgrade facilities for its service department customers, adding a play area for kids, wireless Internet, a coffee bar, a big flat-screen TV, leather chairs, and even a fireplace! Plaza also offers its service customers the option of a loaner car, but as it turns out, the service center's waiting area is so nice that many customers camp out with their laptops and spend their day working at the dealership while repairs are being completed!

Plaza has truly done something remarkable by taking an experience that most of us try to avoid—getting stuck at the dealership when our car needs servicing—and turning it into a Moment of Magic. Almost makes you want to stop in for an oil change, doesn't it? This is akin to movie theaters that flash trivia questions on the screen while you wait for the movie (actually, the previews) to begin, restaurants that bring out complimentary appetizers while you wait for your table, and the entertainment that Disney provides to their theme park guests while they wait in long lines for the various rides.

LESSON: Take something your customers might not like and come up with ways to minimize, or even eliminate, the negative experience.

The Quick Callback

Contrary to what you may think, a WOW! response is not always that difficult to generate. As a matter of fact, in some cases it is pretty darn easy.

A friend of mine was shopping around for a printer who could handle a small publishing project. He called six different places, hoping to talk about the project and get some bids for the job. He was not able to reach a sales representative at any of the six companies, so he left voice messages for all of them. It makes sense that the salespeople might be out selling. However, four of the six printers didn't call back until the next day. One didn't call back at all. It was the sixth sales rep that got the business. He called within a few minutes of the initial call.

For my friend, the quick return call was a WOW! moment, especially compared with the lackadaisical response he received from the other printing companies. That prompt callback immediately gave the sales rep an advantage over his competitors. Despite the fact that the sixth salesperson may have been out making calls, he kept in touch with his home base—and any potential customers who might have surfaced.

LESSON: If you think all WOW moments need to be big, expensive, *amazing*, or even complex—think again. Sometimes something as simple as returning your phone calls (and, for that matter, your e-mail messages) in a prompt manner will generate a WOW! response from your prospects and customers.

Let Us Fix That for You

A while back, an elderly woman walked into one of Aaron Brothers' Dallas stores to buy a picture frame. Before ringing up her purchase for a ready-made frame, the assistant manager suggested that she might want to custom-frame the item (which she'd brought along with her). She declined, explaining that she had recently purchased a custom frame for that item from another frame store, a competitor of Aaron Brothers', and was now disappointed with her choice. Once she'd gotten it home, she explained, it just didn't look right on her wall. "I chose the wrong colors for the matting," she said. "It was my fault." Now she did not want to risk spending the extra money and making another mistake. She just wanted the ready-made frame.

The assistant manager told her that he would like to correct the problem, for free, *even though she had bought the custom frame from a competitor.* Astonished, she agreed to take him up on his offer.

The next day, she brought all the materials in. The assistant manager changed the mats to reflect a different color choice, and the woman left Aaron Brothers, very pleased indeed. Within two weeks, she brought in four additional items to be custom-framed. Aaron Brothers had taken a customer from the competition!

What was their investment? Two pieces of matting—and a culture in which employees are empowered to deliver a WOW service experience!

LESSON: Keep an eye out for simple things you and your team can do to resolve problems that your customers have had with your competitors.

Create a Demanding Customer

If you are truly committed to making the journey to *amazement* with your customers, you and your team should be ready to take aim at the competition in a new way. One of your goals as you move toward *amazement* should be to deliver an experience that is so powerful, compelling, positive, and unique to your organization that, if your customers were to go to your competitor and ask for the same level of service, your competitors would think of the customer as *demanding*.

Virgin Airlines specializes in this. The people at Virgin are constantly finding ways to *add* exciting new elements to the flying experience, like an extensive in-flight selection of on-demand videos and games. And of course, they're doing this at a time when other airlines in the industry are looking for ways to cut the perks. That gives Virgin a huge competitive advantage; their competitors now tend to consider amenities such as videos and games to be a little extreme, given the economic challenges the airline industry is currently facing. In fact, I have a feeling that Virgin has the raised the expectations bar in this area for any number of companies *outside* the airline industry.

Golden Corral, a chain of buffet restaurants and a client of mine, shared a similarly impressive story that is a perfect example of creating a demanding customer. On certain nights, the restaurant serves fried shrimp as a special menu feature. One of the guests came in on a night when the restaurant *wasn't* serving fried shrimp and asked for this particular menu item! The manager could have told the customer that they weren't serving fried shrimp that night, but he didn't. Instead, he personally went into the kitchen and prepared a special order *specifically* for that guest. Talk about raising the bar! Imagine what happens when that guest goes to a competing restaurant and asks for something that's not on the menu. The competition will almost certainly say, "We don't have that on our menu" and might even consider that guest a bit demanding.

LESSON: Ask yourself: "What are *we* doing for our customers that the competition might find just a little extreme?" The answer can give you a competitive advantage that raises the bar, not just in your industry, but also with everyone your customers might do business with.

What a Racket!

When I came across this example of *cult-of-amazement*-like service from the top-tier badminton racket manufacturer Carlton, I knew I had to use it to end this section of the book, because it takes follow-through to the level of high art.

Now, the sport of badminton is a cottage industry, small enough that both good and bad reputations can spread quickly. And that's certainly what happened here. A badminton player wanted to get a favorite limited-edition Carlton racket restrung for an upcoming game. Unfortunately, he had not used the racket in several years, and it had cracked. (Rackets that are idle for a long period of time often have this problem.) The customer called Carlton to try to have the racket fixed and was disappointed to learn that it was beyond repair. To make the situation worse, the model was no longer in production, so it couldn't even be replaced. It was, after all, a limited edition! So Carlton sent along a free replacement—a superb racket known as the Carlton Superlight. Had the story stopped there, Carlton probably would have already found itself with a very happy customer.

In addition to the new racquet, Carlton *also* sent the original racket back—with a new grip—so the customer could hang it in his room for display purposes. Talk about follow-through that was over the top! It *was* his favorite racket, after all. The customer described his experience with Carlton online, writing: *"My bag today holds an AS1 [from Carlton], bought after the breakage, and a MF F1 Ti. After the replacement came, I bought an MF F4 and MF F3 for other members of my family. But perhaps more importantly, I shall be relaying this story to the clubs I go to, and to other players I know. Well done Carlton! I wish to add that I have no connections to Carlton other than as a very happy customer."[6]*

If you ever need a reminder about what evangelism sounds like once a customer has reached the *cult of amazement,* you just read a perfect example of it!

LESSON: Keep an eye out for opportunities to astonish your customer *after* you've solved the initial problem to (or beyond) their satisfaction. The extras or bonuses you throw in may bring your follow-through to the level of WOW! and turn your satisfied customers into customer evangelists!

The Bottom Line

Opportunities to WOW! your customers come in all shapes and sizes. Some of these WOW! moments are going to be a lot easier to pull off than you might think, and some won't even cost that much. Sometimes, all you need to do is manage the details a little differently. Other times, you will be able to deliver a WOW! moment just by recognizing that you have the opportunity to do so. The many different opportunities you will have to WOW! the customer will all be rooted in your long-term mission of striving for *amazement* by dramatically exceeding customer expectations. Whenever you see the opportunity to create a WOW! moment, act on it!

In the next section of the book, I'll share some tools and resources with you that will help you make the journey to *amazement.*

Part Five

CREATING THE CULT OF THE CUSTOMER

Chapter Seventeen

TOOLS FOR SUCCESS

In this section of the book, you'll find the tools you need to start your journey to the *cult of amazement*. Please *use* these tools, because simply *knowing* the concepts is not enough. You have to begin the journey by implementing the information that you have learned in this book. And although using the techniques and completing the exercises doesn't necessarily *guarantee* that you will get to, or stay in, the *cult of amazement*, they will certainly help. These tools are designed to connect you to the fundamentals that will move you forward. They will help you and your employees create awareness of the key concepts, and they will clarify everyone's role in the customer experience strategy.

These guidelines and forms have been adapted from my proprietary training program The Customer Focus™, which my clients have paid thousands of dollars to implement and have been using for many years. I'm not telling you this to impress you; I'm telling you this to impress *upon* you the importance of using and respecting the materials you are about to encounter. These methods work, and they will help you close the gap between what you have learned from the book and what you will actually be doing in your business. (Extra copies of these tools and forms are available at no charge on www.CultOfThe Customer.com.) Unless you are operating as a solo entrepreneur (a Force of One), you should consider implementing these tools in a group setting by taking the following steps:

1. Complete the *What Cult Are You In?* checklists (shown later in this chapter). Doing so will help you assess what cult you are operating in now. *Frequency: Quarterly, to ensure that you are on track or improving.*

2. Then take the *What Cult Are You In?* assessment (See Figure 17.1). Be sure to answer the three questions below the assessment, which will provide clarity on what you and your organization may need to do right now. *Frequency: Quarterly. You may consider performing this assessment monthly for the first three months. Reassess regularly to make sure your organization is not slipping!*

3. Next, complete the *Touch Points Chain Tool* (See Figure 17.2). Recognize that you may have several different chains of touch points and that not all customers have the same experiences. Note that if your customers are online, you will need to identify the touch points or steps they go through as they make transactions through your web site. *Frequency: Quarterly, to remind everyone of the interaction/contact they have with customers on a daily basis.*

4. Next you will work through the *Impact Point Awareness Exercise* (See Figure 17.4). This should be completed for every touch point that is affected by something going on behind the scenes. *Frequency: Quarterly. Note that this tool is the natural follow-up to the Touch Points Chain Tool.*

5. Once you have a basic understanding of your touch points and impact points, it will be time for you to tackle the *Moments of Magic Strategy Grid* (See Figure 17.6). You will be looking at your main touch points and discussing ways to

enhance the customer experience. *Frequency: Quarterly. This tool also ties in with the Touch Points Chain.*

6. Now, let's be realistic. Perfection is not reality. There will be occasional problems, complaints, and obstacles—in other words, Moments of Misery. *The Moments of Misery Strategy Grid* (See Figure 17.8) will help you identify and work through your most common customer problems and complaints. This is an excellent tool to help you work on internal complaints as well. *Frequency: Quarterly. Once again, use this tool in conjunction with the touch point tools. Also, realize that as you work through and resolve the most common issues, others will surface!*

7. Finally, we come to two of my favorite tools: the *Moments of Magic Card* (See Figure 17.10) and the *Moments of Innovation Card* (See Figure 17.11). These cards should be completed by every employee of the company. Don't skip this part! If there is one exercise that has delivered the most results for my clients, it's the use of these two cards on a regular basis. They keep everyone thinking about how to create a great customer experience and how to improve their job and /or the company. The ideal application is for each and every employee in the organization to complete the cards—which takes about five minutes each to do—and then turn them in to a manager (or some other point person). Feedback to the employee is crucial; sharing the best stories and ideas with the team is also important. *Frequency: Weekly. This ensures that every employee is consistently focused on the customer experience.*

All of these tools are part of the process. Once again, using these tools will not guarantee reaching or staying in the *cult of amazement,* but they will surely help. As you embark on this journey, make sure that

- Your organization is out of the *cult of uncertainty.*
- All employees buy into the *cult of alignment.*

- Successes are recognized and celebrated by all employees in the *cult of experience.*
- The success experienced by the employees becomes predictable and the norm in the *cult of ownership.*
- The norm is always excellent, always better than average, and sometimes even a WOW! moment. Only when your people are consistently striving to deliver their very best to each other and to customers can your organization operate in the *cult of amazement.*

The Real Work Begins

Don't just look over the following checklists and exercises. Work through them!

At this point you should have a complete understanding of the five cults and their effect on both employees and customers. You've read dozens of examples and case studies about how individuals and organizations have created *amazement.* As mentioned at the beginning of this chapter, the following exercises and forms are to help move you and your organization forward (or keep you) in the *cult of amazement.* They are also the perfect way to take others along for the journey.

If you work through the checklists, exercises, and forms with the recommended frequency, you will start to see movement toward a customer-focused culture. This takes an ongoing commitment. The checklists and first five exercises are meant to be done quarterly, and they will take time to complete. You should consider doing them.

The *Moments of Magic Card* and *Moments of Innovation Card* will have the most immediate impact. It allows for employees to celebrate their successes and participate in process improvement. It warrants repeating: the success of the *Magic and Innovation cards* will be continuity and feedback. Once a week for each is what is suggested. Everyone must participate. And timely feedback from a manager or supervisor on each and every employee's submission is a non-negotiable.

Remember: As you and your employees travel through these five cults, your customers will be traveling right along with you.

And now it's time to start putting what you know to work!

What Cult Are You In? A Checklist for the Cult of Uncertainty

Customers say: "What's going to happen?"

Employees say: "We aren't sure." There is no consistency.

If you check any of the following, you are at risk of being in the cult of uncertainty.

☐ Service is inconsistent.

☐ Internal processes and communication are inconsistent and disorganized.

☐ Customer retention is not where it should be.

☐ Employees aren't sure what the company's vision and brand promise are.

☐ There is occasional dissension or lack of trust within staff ranks.

☐ Employees and customers are unable to access upper management.

☐ There is no system in place to share best practices.

☐ There is little or no celebration of success.

☐ Employees may be in the wrong job.

☐ Employees feel a lack of appreciation.

☐ There is little or no soft-skills training in communication skills, customer service skills, or the like.

☐ Performance reviews are not executed regularly or with relevance to employee or company goals.

☐ Employees don't feel as though they are part of a team.

☐ Employees have little or no authority to act independently to help the customer.

☐ There is a company-wide lack of motivation and an attitude of indifference.

☐ The company is operations-focused instead of customer-focused.

This is the cult you do *not* want to belong to. Employees and customers tend to have little or no confidence in their experience with the company. Most companies, whether they know it or not, operate inconsistently. Even the great ones occasionally drift into this cult. It takes constant attention, especially to the details, to get out of this cult and stay out.

What Cult Are You In? A Checklist for the Cult of Alignment

Customers say: "Okay, I hear what you're promising. Prove it to me."

Employees say: "Okay, I understand what we're promising. Prove it to me, so that I can prove it to the customer."

If any of the following are not checked, you may not be in the cult of alignment. (Note: Not all need to be checked for you to be in alignment. Some of the following statements may not be applicable to your company or your situation.)

☐ The organization has created a simple and clear vision—a brand promise and/or a mantra.

☐ All employees understand and are able to repeat the mantra and/or brand promise.

☐ The company is hiring and promoting the right person for the right job.

☐ Employee training is not conducted as an afterthought, and it does not focus solely on product and service details. Soft-skills training is included, and a separate and comprehensive training regimen focuses on fulfilling the brand promise to customers.

☐ The organization continuously assesses itself by surveying employees and customers.

☐ Everyone wants to improve. Business as usual is not good enough.

☐ Members of the company commit to improving the experience not just for customers, but for employees as well.

☐ The organization is moving toward being customer-focused, rather than operations-focused.

☐ Both employees and customers know where they're supposed to be going.

☐ Both employees and customers *like* where they're supposed to be going.

When you start focusing on how to repeat *experiences* that support both customers and employees, you are moving out of the cult of alignment and into the cult of experience.

What Cult Are You In? A Checklist for the Cult of Experience

Customers say: "I had a good experience. What will happen next time?"

Employees say: "Wow! It works. I created a good experience for my customer."

If any of the following are not checked, you may not be operating in the cult of experience. (Note: Not all need to be checked for you to be in experience. Some of the following statements may not be applicable to your company or your situation.)

All that you checked in the cult of alignment *plus*

☐ Employees have a personal sense of mission that relates to the job.

☐ The organization has created an experience that relates to that mission.

☐ Employees know what the organization's mantra and/or brand promise is, and they're getting reinforced at some level for fulfilling that mantra.

☐ Employees are starting to feel empowered.

☐ Employees receive positive feedback for trying to do the right thing.

☐ Employees who are involved in creating the organization's virtual or online experience find ways to make the process easy for the *customer*, not just for internal staff members.

☐ Significant numbers of employees are now customer-focused. The customer has begun the process of expecting more from the organization or, at a minimum, expecting more of the same.

☐ Typical day-to-day customer and employee experiences are positive.

When these positive experiences become the norm, confidence starts to build. Once these experiences are predictable and expected, you are moving out of the cult of experience and into the cult of ownership.

What Cult Are You In? A Checklist for the Cult of Ownership

Customers say: "Wow! I had another great experience . . . and another one. There's a pattern here. It's predictable. I like this company."

Employees say: "I know what to do. I have confidence. This is where I belong."

If any of the following are not checked, you may not be operating in the cult of ownership. (Note: Not all need to be checked for you to be in ownership. Some of the following statements may not be applicable to your company or your situation.)

All that you checked in the cults of alignment and experience *plus*

- ☐ Strong levels of employee engagement are the norm (not the exception) in the organization.
- ☐ Higher-than-average retention numbers exist among frontline employees.
- ☐ Formal internal processes have been implemented to empower employees to fix problems.
- ☐ Regular discussion of Moments of Magic types of stories takes place, and there is substantial praise/reward for people who contribute to those discussions.
- ☐ Regular discussion of Moments of Innovation types of ideas occurs, and there is praise/reward for people who contribute to those discussions.
- ☐ Questions that resemble Acceleration Questions are regularly posed during team meetings.
- ☐ Proactive, habitual preparation for those questions takes place among employees.
- ☐ Deep concerns at all levels of the organization for the quality of the customer experience are voiced regularly.
- ☐ Employees have developed the ability to bounce back and recover quickly in situations where there's a challenge with a customer by fixing the problem with a sense of urgency and with the right attitude.

When customers come to expect not just positive, but above-average responses from you, and start recommending you to others as a result, you are moving out of the cult of ownership and into the *cult of amazement.*

What Cult Are You In? A Checklist for the *Cult of Amazement*

Customers say: "This company is great. You *must* do business with them!" They become your evangelists!

Employees say: "I love working here!" They tell everyone how great the company is. They become your evangelists!

If any of the following are not checked, you may not be operating in the *cult of amazement.* (Note: Not all of these need to be checked for you to be in *amazement.* Some of the following statements may not be applicable to your company or your situation.)

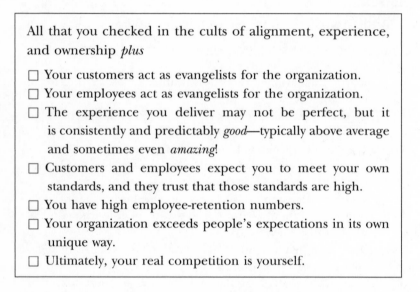

All that you checked in the cults of alignment, experience, and ownership *plus*

☐ Your customers act as evangelists for the organization.

☐ Your employees act as evangelists for the organization.

☐ The experience you deliver may not be perfect, but it is consistently and predictably *good*—typically above average and sometimes even *amazing*!

☐ Customers and employees expect you to meet your own standards, and they trust that those standards are high.

☐ You have high employee-retention numbers.

☐ Your organization exceeds people's expectations in its own unique way.

☐ Ultimately, your real competition is yourself.

Being in the *cult of amazement* means you have mastered alignment, experience, and ownership. *Staying* in *amazement* is the true test; it is very easy to fall out of *amazement* once you have entered it. One employee or one mistake can make a customer uncertain. Should that happen, you must restore confidence. When customers know they can count on you, even if there are problems, you will always have their loyalty. The customer loyalty formula is:

Great Service + Confidence = Loyalty

And loyalty can eventually turn into evangelism!

What Cult Are You In?

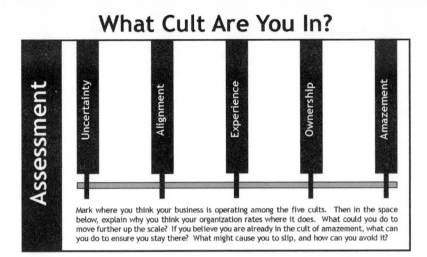

Assessment

Uncertainty | Alignment | Experience | Ownership | Amazement

Mark where you think your business is operating among the five cults. Then in the space below, explain why you think your organization rates where it does. What could you do to move further up the scale? If you believe you are already in the cult of amazement, what can you do to ensure you stay there? What might cause you to slip, and how can you avoid it?

What is your current cult, and why?

What do you need to do to move to the next cult, if you are not already in the cult of amazement?

What must you do to ensure that you do not slip to a lower cult?

Figure 17.1   What Cult Are You in? Assessment

Copyright © Shep Hyken, Shepard Presentations, LLC,
www.CultOfTheCustomer.com.

The Touch Points Chain

OVERVIEW: Managing the touch points is critical. The first step is to know what touch points your cusotmers experience. Every customer will go through a chain of touch points. Depending on your business, different customers may go through a different sequence of events. Each of these touch points are like links of a chain.

Moments of Truth - According to Jan Carlzon, a Moment of Truth is any time a customer comes into contact with any aspect of a business, ***however remote,*** and has an opportunity to form an impression.

Touch Points - Touch points are Moments of Truth, the points of contact where a customer physically encounters the business in some way, usually people-to-people contact.

Impact Points - Impact points are the behind-the-scenes systems or operations that ultimately impact the customer's experience.

INSTRUCTIONS: Using the form on the next page, record the chain of touch points that occur in your business. Use the space below the chain if you have more touch points than there are boxes next to the chain. An example is below.

A SAMPLE TOUCH POINTS—MOMENTS OF TRUTH CHAIN

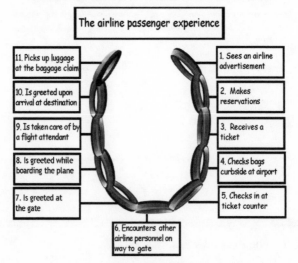

The airline passenger experience

11. Picks up luggage at the baggage claim

10. Is greeted upon arrival at destination

9. Is taken care of by a flight attendant

8. Is greeted while boarding the plane

7. Is greeted at the gate

6. Encounters other airline personnel on way to gate

1. Sees an airline advertisement

2. Makes reservations

3. Receives a ticket

4. Checks bags curbside at airport

5. Checks in at ticket counter

Figure 17.2   The Touch Points Chain Sample

The Touch Points Chain

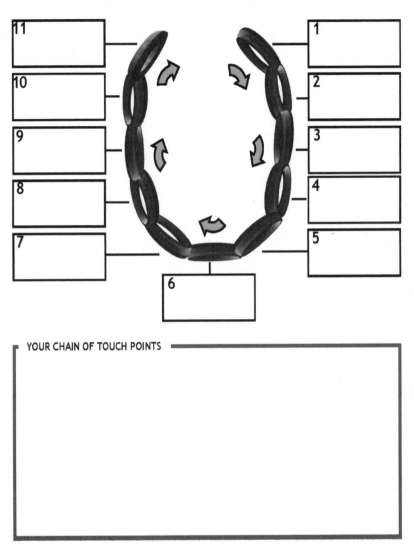

YOUR CHAIN OF TOUCH POINTS

Figure 17.3 The Touch Points Chain Tool
Copyright © Shep Hyken, Shepard Presentations, LLC,
www.CultOfTheCustomer.com.

Impact Point Awareness Exercise

OVERVIEW: Impact points support touch points. Being aware of the impact points will help support your efforts to create an amazing customer experience.

INSTRUCTIONS: Record the behind-the-scenes impact points for two touch points you listed on the previous page. An example is provided.

This exercise should be completed for every touch point that is supported by behind-the-scenes impact points.

TOUCH POINT:

Passenger checks bags curbside at the airport.

IMPACT POINT:

1. The baggage gets routed to a handler.
2. Bags are placed in the correct area for the correct flight.
3. Bags loaded onto the plane.
4. Bags are taken off the plane upon arrival.
5. Bags are routed to the baggage claim area.
6. Bags are put onto the carousel by a handler.
7. Bags come out and are picked up by passenger. (Actually, this is a touch point.)

Figure 17.4   Impact Point Awareness Exercise Sample
Copyright © Shep Hyken, Shepard Presentations, LLC,
www.CultOfTheCustomer.com.

Impact Point Awareness

TOUCH POINT:

IMPACT POINT:

TOUCH POINT:

IMPACT POINT:

Figure 17.5   Impact Point Awareness Exercise

Copyright © Shep Hyken, Shepard Presentations, LLC, www.CultOfTheCustomer.com.

Moments of Magic Strategy Grid

OVERVIEW: To create a great customer experience, you must create Moments of Magic from the touch points. Take a look at the touch points your customers experience and come up with ways that will improve the experience. Sometimes the Touch Points will be amazing. At a minimum, come up with ways to make them better than average.

INSTRUCTIONS: Review your touch points. Select three points of contact with your customer and, using the grid on the next page, suggest ways that those touch points can be turned into Moments of Magic. Also include the outcome or impact that doing so could have on your customers and/or business. A sample in below.

This exercise should eventually be completed for all Touch Points.

TOUCH POINT	MOMENTS OF MAGIC STRATEGY	OUTCOME
Receptionist answers the phone.	Currently, the receptionist answers the phone this way: "widget Blue." From now on we answer the phone with an enthusiastic voice saying: "Good monrning (or afternoon), WidgetBlue. This is ...., may I help you!	We want to be a great company that people like to do business with, which means they have to like us as people. Let's personalize the greeting. Let the customer know he/she is talking to a person, not a company.

Figure 17.6   Moments of Magic Strategy Grid Sample

Moments of Magic Strategy Grid

TOUCH POINT	MOMENTS OF MAGIC STRATEGY	OUTCOME
1		
2		
3		

Figure 17.7   Moments of Magic Strategy Grid

Copyright © Shep Hyken, Shepard Presentations, LLC,
www.CultOfTheCustomer.com.

Moments of Misery Strategy Grid

OVERVIEW: Moments of Misery are going to happen. It is how you handle them that will make the difference between a satisfied customer and a loyal customer. When you have a problem, don't just fix it. Focus on what you can do to renew the confidence of the customer. You want them to know they can count on you.

INSTRUCTIONS: List some Moments of Misery within your company. Using the grid on the next page, describe the most common complaints or problems that you hear from your customers. How often do they occur, and what can you do to prevent them? Try to be as creative and proactive with your solutions as possible. A sample is below.

NOTE: Consider going through this exercise once a month for six months. then, switch to once each quarter. Your goal is to eliminate problems/complaints. Realize that as you eliminate them, others will come up and take their place.

MOMENT OF MISERY	HOW OFTEN?	PREVENTION / SOLUTION
Customers complain calls are not returned very quickly—sometimes as long as two and three days.	Daily. We have 20 customer service reps. We are probably only hearing from a fraction of our customers. We hear this 8 to 10 times a day, so the number is probably' much higher.	First, we need to determine why it takes so long to get the calls returned. Second, are we properly staffed to handle the calls? Let's do on analysis. Third, let's put a policy in place that requires all calls returned within four business hours. Easy to do. No excuse not to.

Figure 17.8   Moments of Misery Strategy Grid Sample
Copyright © Shep Hyken, Shepard Presentations, LLC,
www.CultOfTheCustomer.com.

Moments of Misery Strategy Grid

MOMENT OF MISERY	HOW OFTEN?	PREVENTION / SOLUTION
1		
2		
3		

Figure 17.9   Moments of Misery Strategy Grid

Copyright © Shep Hyken, Shepard Presentations, LLC,
www.CultOfTheCustomer.com.

Moments of Magic Card

OVERVIEW: People can relate to a story, especially when it is their own. Part of the success of any customer service/experience program is to have all employees on board, with the customer always in mind. When employees are sharing their stories on a regular schedule (once a week), you know that they are at least thinking of how they can deliver extraordinary service.

INSTRUCTIONS: Fill out the the Moments of Magic form below with one of your own personal examples. This exercise should be completed once a week. Unless you are operating as a solo entrepreneur, these cards should be turned into a manager.

Note to manager: Give feedback. Share great stories with others in the company.

A *Moment of Truth* is any time someone comes into contact with us or our company. Individually, these contacts are referred to as touch points.

It can be good, it can be bad, or it can be just average ("OK" or satisfactory).

A *Moment of Magic* is anything that is better than just "OK". Sometimes, it's even amazing.

Briefly describe a *Moment of Magic* that you created for either a customer of fellow employee. This can come from resolving a complaint, helping a customer in need or simply creating an amazing customer experience.

Name:

Manager Comment:

Figure 17.10 Moments of Magic Card

Copyright © Shep Hyken, Shepard Presentations, LLC, www. CultOfTheCustomer.com.

Moments of Innovation Card

OVERVIEW: This exercise can keep your team thinking about how to always be improving their company, their individual responsibilities, and themselves. It is all about process improvement and creating a better customer experience.

INSTRUCTIONS: Fill out the the the *Moments of Innovation,* form below with one of your own personal examples. This is an exercise that should be completed once every week.

Moments of
Innovation™

Name:

A *Moment of innovation* is any time an employee comes up with an idea or suggestion to make a change to the job, a procedure, or anything that could increase production, decrease cost or *positively impact the customer.*

The end result is some type of change or improvement that makes things better, giving employees input in the way things are done and giving them a say in the company.

Sometimes, being prompted to brainstorm ideas is the best way to think creatively and come up with some incredible suggestions! Use this card to create your own *Moment of Innovation.*

Manager Comment:

Figure 17.11   Moments of Innovation Card

Copyright © Shep Hyken, Shepard Presentations, LLC, www. CultOfTheCustomer.com.

DOWNLOAD THESE FORMS!

You can download clean copies of all of the tools and forms in this chapter at www.CultOfTheCustomer.com.

There you will find clean copies of these valuable resources—and much more. As I come up with updates and new concepts that revolve around *The Cult of the Customer,* I will place them on the web site. Check in often!

Epilogue

Late on a Friday night, Mike was getting ready to take a surprise walk around WidgetBlue's all-but-deserted factory floor.

Over the years, Mike had developed a habit of wandering around every imaginable nook and cranny of the company—the executive offices, the employee lounge, the mail room, and yes, even the factory floor—at times when people weren't expecting him.

He wasn't trying to sneak up on anyone. Mike was just always looking for new people he could meet, new ideas he could brainstorm, and new spirits he could lift. Truth be told, he now thought of himself as more of a cheerleader than as the CEO of the company.

Tonight, Mike thought he'd introduce himself to the newest member of the WidgetBlue team, Walt Williams, who had just been hired to the janitorial staff. Walt had been trained and gone through his initial orientation the previous week. He had started his very first shift at four that afternoon and was responsible for cleanup, shutdown, and lockup that night.

As Mike made his way down to the floor, he heard a strange, low sound, like someone grumbling. He walked quietly and purposefully toward the source of the sound, and the words from the shop floor became clearer and clearer to him:

"What difference does it make . . . what difference does it make . . . what difference does it make. . . . "

Mike followed the sound. He stepped to within 20 feet of Walt, who was completely unaware of Mike's presence. Walt was sweeping diligently, with every stroke, he was repeating the same forlorn phrase.

"What difference does it make . . . what difference does it make . . . what difference does it make. . . . "

"Actually, that's not our mantra anymore," Mike said, smiling.

Walt wheeled around. His eyes were wide, and his face froze in alarm.

"Mr. Hardhead!" Walt gasped.

"Actually, nobody in the company calls me that," Mike explained. "Just call me Mike. Pleased to meet you."

Walt was literally speechless as he shook Mike's hand. He tried to form some words but couldn't manage to do so. A long moment passed.

"I didn't mean to startle you, Walt," Mike continued apologetically. "I just wanted to introduce myself and see how your first day was going. You're not in any trouble, I promise. Would you mind coming up to my office for a moment? I have something I'd like to give you."

Dumbfounded, the new janitor started to follow the CEO toward his vast, broad-windowed, third-floor office, which looked down majestically on the very factory floor where Walt had been sweeping and muttering helplessly to himself just moments before.

"There was a time," Mike explained from behind his huge mahogany desk, "when the chips were down for me, and I found myself repeating precisely those words you were just saying down on the factory floor."

"So you're really not going to fire me?"

"Fire you? I'm certainly not about to fire someone for doing exactly what I used to do. Believe me. Sometimes I said those words out loud. Sometimes I said them silently, to myself. But there was definitely a time in my life when I said them a great deal. Once, my old mentor, Harlan Love, heard me saying them. He took me aside, wrote something down on a sheet of paper, and handed that sheet to me. On that sheet he had recorded the wisdom of a very great man. Now that I've taken over Harlan's old job, I've passed along the same wisdom to every new hire we've ever brought on in this organization—every senior executive, every designer, every factory worker, and everyone who's ever pushed a broom on the shop floor. Would you like to read what's on the sheet Harlan gave me that day?"

Walt gulped. "I guess so, Mr. Hardh—er, Mike. But if I may, let me just explain why I was saying what I was saying. You see, I've wanted to work in this industry for years, but after months of knocking on doors at every company I could think of, all I could land was this janitor's job. It seemed so far away from the customers, so far away from the design and marketing work I wanted to do, the problems I wanted to solve, and. . . . ''

Mike smiled and held up a single finger in front of his lips. Walt stopped talking.

Mike reached into his coat pocket and pulled out a yellowed, folded sheet of paper. He unfolded it carefully and handed it to Walt.

The page was filled with the large, careful block printing of someone with aged, but steady, handwriting. Here is what it said:

"If a man is called to be a streetsweeper, he should sweep streets even as Michelangelo painted, or Beethoven composed music, or Shakespeare wrote poetry. He should sweep streets so well that all the host of heaven and earth will pause to say, here lived a great streetsweeper who did his job well.''—Martin Luther King Jr.

Walt stared at the sheet. He read it over several times.

Then Mike said, "That's what we have to remember here, every day, Walt. If we each do our jobs the way Michelangelo did his job, the way Beethoven did his job, the way Shakespeare did his job, then we can't help but *amaze* each other—and if we make a habit of *amazing* each other, then we will inevitably end up *amazing* the customer. That goes for me. It goes for you. It goes for everyone. We're all playing by exactly the same rules.

"And by the way, Walt," Mike continued, "you should know that my chief operating officer started out here seven years ago doing exactly the job that you're doing tonight: sweeping the factory floor and keeping this place so clean that people felt proud to show up for work each morning. Has it ever occurred to you, Walt, that a factory shop floor is a great place to learn about exactly how a company solves problems for its customers?"

That night, Mike and Walt swept the factory floor together— and talked long into the night about the company's customers, products, markets, and goals. By the end of the night—and it was a long and very pleasant one, indeed—Walt had embarked on a journey that never ends: the journey toward the cult of the customer.

The Final Keeper

No matter what you do, always do your best. It is the consistent effort to be *amazing* that creates confidence. When you make a habit of *amazing* the people you work with, you will inevitably end up *amazing* your customers . . . and these *amazing* experiences will turn your satisfied customers into customer evangelists!

Notes

Chapter 2 Do You Need This Book?

1. Theodore Levitt, *The Marketing Imagination.* New York: Free Press, 1986.
2. Bain & Company (www.bain.com/bainweb/publications/publica-tions_detail.asp?id=25271&menu_url=publications_results.asp).
3. Walker Loyalty Report Executive Summary, September 2007.

Chapter 3 The Three Forces

1. Andy McCue, "CRM investments failing to foster customer loyalty," Silicon.com, July 2005.
2. Mark Stevens, *Extreme Management: What They Teach at Harvard Business School's Advanced Management Program.* New York: Warner Books, 2001.

Chapter 4 Uncertainty

1. Megan Burns, "Customer experience spending intensifies in 2008" (www.forrester.com/Research/Document/Excerpt/0,7211,45134,00.html).
2. Mark Stevens, Extreme Management: What They Teach at Harvard Business School's Advanced Management Program. New York: Warner Books, 2001.

3. Newgistics Intelligent Logistics Management Newsletter, September 2004.

Chapter 5 Alignment

1. Carla Heaton and Rick Guzzo, *Delivering on the Brand Promise: Making Every Employee a Brand Manager, Aligning Human Capital Strategy with Brand Strategy* (www.lippincotmercer.com/publications/articles.shtml).

Chapter 6 Experience

1. TARP Worldwide, "The Truth according to TARP," September 2006 (www.newtoncomputing.com/zips/basicfacts.pdf).

Chapter 7 Ownership

1. Doug Henschen, "Case Study: Keep Track of the Bright Ideas," *Intelligent Enterprise*, July 18, 2005.
2. Jennifer Vilaga, "Employee Innovator Runner-up: Zappos," *Fast Company Magazine*, October 2005.
3. Zappos.com, *Zappos Culture Book*, 2007.
4. Ibid.
5. Ibid.
6. Bill Taylor, Game Changer Blog, www.HarvardBusiness.org, May 19, 2008.
7. Zappos.com, *Zappos Culture Book*, 2007.
8. Dave Chaffey, "Amazon Case Study," DaveChaffey.com, March 2008.

Chapter 8 Amazement

1. Judith McGinnis, "Melting Dad's heart," *Wichita Falls Times Record News*, June 8, 2008.
2. www.biggreenegg.com/history.html.
3. Jeffrey Pfeiffer, quoted in an interview on Guy Kawasaki's blog How to Change the World (www.blog.guykawasaki.com/), July 13, 2007.
4. An Tien Hsieh and Wen Ting Chang, "The Effect of Consumer Participation on Price Sensitivity," *Journal of Consumer Affairs* 38, 2004.
5. TARP Worldwide (www.tarp.com).
6. Robin Thompson, "Secrets to Keeping Good Employees" (www.RobinThompson.com).
7. "Best Places to Launch a Career, 2007" www.businessweek.com/careers/content/sep2007/ca20070913_595536.htm.
8. "The GCSU iPod Story," http://ipod.gcsu.edu.

Chapter 9 What the Journey Looks Like from the Inside

1. Robert Spector and Patrick McCarthy, *The Nordstrom Way to Customer Service Excellence: A Handbook for Implementing Great Service in Your Organization.* Hoboken, NJ: John Wiley & Sons, 2005.
2. Eugene B. Habecker, *The Other Side of Leadership.* Scripture Pr Pubns., 1987.
3. www.brainyquote.com/quotes/authors/j/joe_paterno.html.
4. Don Wainwright, in a 2001 speech before the National Association of Manufacturers. (Jack Welch has since retired from General Electric.)
5. Don Wainwright, quoted in John S. McClenahen, "Executive Word— Don't Be Passive on Public Policy," *IndustryWeek,* May 1, 2002.
6. Don Wainwright, quoted in Gregory P. Smith, "Building Trust: A Key Element in Worker Productivity," www.salesvantage.com, 2003.
7. Morris Panner, "Huddle Up!," *Fast Company* magazine, November 2000.
8. Spector and McCarthy, *The Nordstrom Way.*

Chapter 10 What the Journey Looks Like from the Outside

1. www.Wegmans.com.
2. www.WeLoveWegmans.blogspot.com.
3. We Love Wegmans group on Flickr.com.
4. www.StarrySteph.blogspot.com.
5. Robert Hargrove, *E-leader: Reinventing Leadership in a Connected Economy.* New York: Basic Books, 2001.
6. www.Virgin.com.

Chapter 11 Launching the Amazement Revolution

1. Jan Carlzon, *Moments of Truth.* Cambridge, MA: Ballinger Publishing Company, 1987.

Chapter 14 Opportunity Knocks

1. http://MummyMusings.wordpress.com.

Chapter 15 Proactive Service and Follow-Through

1. "Customer Service Champs," *BusinessWeek,* March 5, 2007.

Chapter 16 The Art of WOW

1. http://goodonpaper.org.
2. Libraries and Life, http://curtisrogers.blogspot.com/2008/01/apple-store-amazing-customer-service.html.

3. http://dragonforged.com/blog/2007/08/dhl-goes-way-beyond-customer-s.html.

4. http://dylanschiemann.com/2007/11/10/amazing-service-from-photojojo/.

5. Rob Baedeker, "New Resource Bank Has Amazing Service," *San Francisco Chronicle*, December 17, 2007.

6. www.badmintoncentral.com/forums/showthread.php?t=13610).

Acknowledgments

Where do I begin? First, let me thank *you*, the reader, for taking the time to read this book. I have put my heart and soul into creating this book for you. I sincerely hope that you find it to be a valuable investment of your time and that you will use the ideas, concepts, and strategies to create *amazing* experiences for your customers and the people you work with.

A big thank you goes to my colleagues: speakers, trainers, consultants, and authors. These friends have inspired and influenced me. With their vast knowledge and experience, they are the greatest people to share and debate ideas with.

All of my clients, in their own way, have helped me write this book. I am lucky to have worked with some of the greatest organizations in the world. Every client and every speech is like a new adventure. I get to hear leaders of the corporate world share their beliefs and visions for their companies and their people. Thank you, as you have all taught me valuable lessons.

Thanks to my new friends at Wiley. The support from their team has made writing this book a pleasure.

Special thanks to Brandon Toropov, my editor, who took my notes and tape-recorded words and turned them into a readable and effective form.

And there is my family: my wife, Cindy, and my three kids, Brian, Alex, and Casey. My business has a crazy schedule that takes me all over the world to meet with clients and speak at their meetings and conferences. And even when I was home, supposedly not working, I was still spending evenings writing this book. My family has always been incredibly supportive. Thank you for the encouragement, enthusiasm, and unconditional love you give me. Right back at you!

About the Author

Who Is Shep Hyken?

Shep Hyken, CSP, CPAE, is a speaker and author who works with companies and organizations who want to build loyal relationships with their customers and employees. His articles have been read in hundreds of publications, and he is the author of *Moments of Magic* and *The Loyal Customer.* He is also the creator of *The Customer Focus*™ program, which helps clients develop a customer service culture and loyalty mind-set.

In 1983, Shep founded Shepard Presentations, LLC, and since then has worked with hundreds of clients, ranging from Fortune 100 organizations to companies with fewer than 50 employees. His clients include American Airlines, AAA, Anheuser-Busch, AT&T, Aetna, Abbott Laboratories, and American Express—and that's just a few of the A's!

Shep Hyken's most requested programs focus on customer service, customer loyalty, internal service, customer relations, and the customer experience. He is known for his high-energy presentations, which combine important information with entertainment (humor and magic) to create exciting programs for his audiences.

The Council of Peers Award for Excellence (CPAE) is the National Speakers Association's Speaker Hall of Fame award for lifetime achievement in the area of platform and/or speaking excellence. The international designation for certified speaking professionals (CSP) is awarded to individuals for certain achievements and education in the speaking profession.

Shep Hyken, CSP, CPAE
Shepard Presentations, LLC
Phone: (314)692–2200
shep@hyken.com
www.hyken.com

Index

Aaron Brothers, 199–200

Accelerator questions, 65–66, 71

Airlines
  force within, 23
  Moments of Truth, 125–126
  recovery experiences, 166–168

Alignment, cult of, 43–52
  benefits of, 46–47
  checklist for, 210
  creating of, 50
  examples, 45–46
  external, 12
  internal, 14
  keepers about, 52
  signs of, 50–51
  staying in, 136
  transition from uncertainty to, 32, 44
  WidgetBlue story, 48–50

Allen, Paul, 116

Allies, in amazement, 134

Amazement, cult of, 17, 26, 73–85
  checklist for, 214
  examples, 73–76, 81–83
  external, 13–14

forgiveness and, 76–77
internal, 15–16
keepers about, 84–85
price and, 78–81
signs of, 84
WidgetBlue story, 77–78, 83

Amazement, external march to, 105–121
  critical pathways, 118–120
  examples, 106–120
  keepers about, 120–121

Amazement, internal march to, 89–103
  critical pathways, 98–99
  examples, 92–102
  keepers about, 103
  modeling Moments of Magic®, 89–92

Amazement, value of, 8–11

Amazement revolution, 123–138
  evaluating progress toward, 123–124
  exercises to encourage, 132–133
  force of many and, 124, 135–136
  force of one and, 124, 133

Amazement, revolution (*continued*)
  force within and, 124, 133–135
  human resource strategies, 131–132
  journey to amazement and, 124
  keepers about, 137–138
  operations- or customer-focus, 129–132
  touch points and impact points, 124–128
Amazon.com, 70, 186
American Express, 154
Apple Computer, 77, 82–83, 194
Aristotle, 63
"Art of Wow" pathway
  examples, 68–70
  experiences of, 189–202
  external march to amazement, 120
  internal march to amazement, 98–99
Attitude, importance of employee's, 158–159
Austin, Phyllis, 149
Auto repair story, 160–161
Avis Rent-a-Car, 45

Badminton racket story, 201–202
Beatles, 45–46
Big Green Egg, 73–76
Black, Terry, 39
Branson, Richard, 110
  background, 113–116
  critical pathways, 118–120
  Virgin Group and, 111–113, 117–118
Brio restaurant, 143–144
Brown, Glen, 146–147
Business Week, 80, 107

Cabdriver story, 24–26
Calls, importance of returning promptly, 198–199
Cameron Mitchell restaurants, 150
Carlton rackets, 201–202
Carlzon, Jan, 125–126, 144

Cell phone industry, 60
Challenger Outplacement Council, 80
Checketts, Dave, 154–156
Circle K, 101
Confidence, from confirmation, 185–186
Confirmations, to create confidence, 185–186
Consistency
  cult of uncertainty and, 11
  forms of uncertainty, 38–40
  importance of, 10
  journey to amazement and, 17, 123
  keepers about, 41–42
  most businesses and, 32–38
  signs of uncertainty, 40–41
  WidgetBlue story, 33–40
Conversation, with clients, 147–148
Critical pathways
  internal march to amazement, 98–99
  Virgin Group, 118–120
Cults. *See also specific cults*
  summarized, 11–16, 31
  use of term, 10
  What Cult Are You In? checklists, 206, 210–214
Customer experiences, improving quality of, 7
Customer Focus training program, 205
Customer Respect Group, 47
Customer-focused thinking, 129–131
  human resource strategies to encourage, 131–132
  moving to, 162–163
Customers
  creating demanding, 200–201
  importance of, 3–4
  keeping in touch with, 183–184
  purpose of business and, 5–7
  recovery experiences and, 153–169

satisfied versus loyal, 7–11, 17
as those with whom you do
business, 6
uncertainty and, 40–41

DaVita, 77
Dell, 186
DHL, 195–196
DiJulius, John, 150
Disney, Walt, 131
Disney organization, 79–81, 130–131, 179–180
Doctor Who, 115
Dress code, at Wainwright
Industries, 94–95

E-mail
importance of getting customer
addresses, 146
sending, to instill confidence, 186
Employees. *See also* Amazement,
internal march to
creating positive work
environment for, 156
cult of alignment and, 51
cult of ownership and, 63–72
customer-focus and, 123–138
as evangelists, 15–16
treating like customers, 56, 90,
180–181
uncertainty and, 40–41
Enterprise Rent-A-Car, 48
Evangelists, creating, 73–85
customers as, 13–14, 17
employees as, 15–16
examples, 73–76, 81–83
forgiveness and, 76–77
keepers about, 84–85
price and, 78–81
signs of, 84
WidgetBlue story, 77–78, 83
Experience, cult of, 53–62
checklist for, 212
examples, 57–59
external, 12
internal, 15

keepers about, 61–62
momentum and, 54–55
signs of, 60–61
WidgetBlue story, 55–57

Fisher, Ed, 76
Follow-up, importance of, 145–147.
See also "Proactive culture"
pathway
Force of many, 20, 24–26
journey to amazement and, 134,
135–136
mantras and, 47
Force of one, 19, 20–22
journey to amazement and, 124,
133
mantras and, 46
Force within, 19–20, 22–23
journey to amazement and, 124,
133–135
mantras and, 46, 49
Forgiveness, amazement and, 76–77
Frank the cabdriver story, 21–22

Gabriele, Scott, 101
Genie story, 3–4
Georgia College and State
University, 83
Ginsberg, Scott, 147–148
Glenn, Edmund, 177–178
Goals, differ from purpose, 6
Golden Corral, 200–201
Groswald, Vicki, 182–183

Habecker, Eugene B., 90
Hardin, Hord, 172–173
Hsieh, Tony, 69–70

Impact points, 124–128, 133
defined, 126–127
Impact Point Awareness Exercise,
207, 218–219
ways to improve, 127–128
Innovation, 66–67
In Search of Excellence (Peters and
Waterman), xiii

Insurance Carrier Scorecard, 47
Internal customers, as those with
    whom you work, 6
iPod, 82–83

Johnson & Johnson, 165–166

Keepers
    amazement revolution, 137–138
    cult of alignment, 52
    cult of amazement, 84–85
    cult of experience, 61–62
    cult of ownership, 71–72
    cult of uncertainty, 41–42
    external march to amazement,
        120–121
    internal march to amazement,
        103
    purpose of business, 17
    service forces, 26–27
Kelleher, Herb, 77
Keynote Competitive Research, 47

Levitt, Theodore, 6, 11, 17
"Little things mean a lot" pathway
    experiences of, 143–152
    external march to amazement, 119
    internal march to amazement, 98
Liu, Peter, 197
L.L. Bean, 186
Long-distance phone service story,
    168–169
Loyal customers, 8–11, 17
Loyalty programs, 194–195

Mantras, importance of, 43–52
    benefits, 46–47
    creating, 50
    cult of experience and, 61
    examples, 45–46
    keepers about, 52
    at Mid-America Motorworks, 99–
        100
    signs of, 50–51
    WidgetBlue story, 48–50
Marcellino Ristorante, 193–194

Marketing Imagination, The (Levitt), 6
Mid-America Motorworks, 99–100
Miracle on 34th Street (film), 177–178
Missouri Baptist Medical Center, 149
Moments of Innovation™, 66, 71,
    72
    Card, 207, 225
Moments of Magic®, 8–11, 17, 66–
    67, 71, 72
    Card, 207, 224
    modeling of, 89–92
    Strategy Grid, 206, 220–221
Moments of Misery®, 25
    preventable causes of, 130, 136
    Strategy Grid, 207, 222–223
Moments of Truth, 125–126
Montemurro, Gerald, 193–194
Morton's Steakhouse, 194–195
Moseley, Harman, 163–164
Movement in right direction. See
    Alignment, cult of
Murdoch, Rupert, 105

Name, importance of using client's,
    148–149
Neiman Marcus, 145, 150–151
New Resource Bank, 197
Nintendo Wii, 192–193
Nordstrom, 102, 166
Nordstrom, Bruce, 89, 102

Oldfield, Mike, 115
Online sellers
    cult of experience, 59
    loyalty and, 33
Open.com, 100–101
"Opportunity knocks" pathway
    experiences of, 171–178
    external march to amazement,
        119
    internal march to amazement, 98
Outback Steakhouse, 45
Ownership, cult of, 63–72
    checklist for, 213
    examples, 66–70
    external, 12–13

internal, 15
keepers about, 71–72
signs of, 71
WidgetBlue story, 64–67

Panera Bread, 106–107
Panner, Morris, 100–101
Paterno, Joe, 92
PayPal, 58–59, 70
Peters, Tom, xiii
Photojojo.com, 196–197
Plaza Motors, 173–174, 197–198
Pogue, David, 177
Predictability, importance of,
    63–72
  examples, 66–70
  keepers about, 71–72
  signs of, 71
  WidgetBlue story, 64–67
Pre-event touch, 181–182
Presentation, importance of, 143–
    144
Price, cult of amazement and, 78–81
"Proactive culture" pathway
  experiences of, 179–187
  external march to amazement,
    119–120
  internal march to amazement, 98
"Problem solving" pathway
  experiences of, 153–169
  external march to amazement,
    119
  internal march to amazement, 98
Progressive Car Insurance, 47
Purpose of business, 5–7, 17

Records, keeping of what ought to
    happen, 134
Recovery. *See* "Problem solving"
    pathway
Return policy, of Wegmans, 107
Ritz-Carlton hotels, 24–26, 45, 147–
    148, 180–181
Roethke, Theodore, 127
Roselman, Irv, 151
Routines, importance of, 100–101

Santa Clause paradox, 177–178
Scandinavian Airlines, 125–126, 144
Schultz, Howard, 186–187
"Second-chance insurance policy,"
    84
Segway, 174–175
Service forces, 19–27
  force of many, 20, 24–26
  force of one, 19, 20–22
  force within, 19–20, 22–23
  keepers about, 26–27
Sex Pistols, 115
Skywest Airlines, 167–168
Southwest Airlines, 77, 184
St. Louis Blues hockey team, 154–
    156
Starbucks, 57–58, 186–187
Staying in touch, importance of,
    144–152
Suggestion program, at Wainwright
    Industries, 95–96
Super Smokers BBQ, 39
Swinmum, Nick, 68

Thank you notes, 145, 149
Thomas, Andrew, 180
Thrifty Foods, 175–177
Timbuk2, 190–192
Tony's restaurant, St. Louis, 81–82
Tools for success
  benefits of, 213–215
  Impact Point Awareness, 206,
    218–219
  Internet access for, 206, 226
  Moments of Innovation™ card,
    207, 225
  Moments of Magic® card, 207,
    224
  Moments of Magic® Strategy
    Grid, 206, 220–221
  Moments of Misery® Strategy
    Grid, 207, 222–223
  Touch Points Chain, 206,
    216–217
  What Cult Are You In? checklists,
    210–214

Tools for success (*continued*)
Touch points, 124–128
   defined, 125–126
   exercises for, 132–133
   Touch Points Chain, 206, 216–217
   ways to improve, 127–128
Touch-ups, watching for needed,
      149–150
Training
   cult of alignment, 51
   importance of, 157–159
   uncertainty and, 40–41
   at Wainwright Industries, 95
Tylenol, 165–166

Uncertainty, cult of, 31–42
   checklist for, 210
   external, 11–12
   forms of uncertainty, 38–40
   internal, 14
   journey to amazement and, 123
   keepers about, 41–42
   signs of, 40–41
   transition to alignment, 32, 44
   as way most business is done, 32–
      38
   WidgetBlue story, 33–40

Vendors, keeping in touch with,
      183–184

Veriza, Sima and Marcellino, 193–
      194
Virgin Group, 111–120, 200
Vittert, Mark, 151
Volkswagen, 45

Wainwright, Don, 93–99
Wainwright Industries, 92–99
Wegmans, 107–109
Welch, Jack, 94
What Cult Are You In? checklists,
      206, 210–214
What's the Secret? (DiJulius), 150
White, Harl, 173–174
WidgetBlue stories
   cult of alignment, 48–50
   cult of amazement, 77–78, 83
   cult of experience, 55–57
   cult of ownership, 64–67
   cult of uncertainty, 33–40
Wow, art of. *See* "Art of Wow"
      pathway

Xerox, 159
XTRA Lease, 164–165

Yager, Mike, 99–100
Yes, policy of saying, 150–151

Zappos, 67–70, 186, 189–190